LIFE
Between the
KEYS

THE (MIS)ADVENTURES
OF THE 5 BROWNS

☰5 BROWNS

ILLUSTRATED BY
AARON GRIEGO

DOVE
BOOKS

Copyright © 2009 The 5 Browns & Dove Books, Inc.

The opinions expressed in this book are those of the author of this book and do not necessarily reflect the views of the publisher or its affiliates.

ISBN-10: 1-59777-589-4
ISBN-13: 978-1-59777-589-2
Library of Congress Cataloging-In-Publication Data Available

Book Design by: Marti Lou Critchfield

Printed in the United States of America

Dove Books, Inc.
9465 Wilshire Boulevard, Suite 840
Beverly Hills, CA 90212

10 9 8 7 6 5 4 3 2

TABLE OF CONTENTS

INTRODUCTION

BY JOEL DIAMOND

The phrase "one of a kind" is used very loosely in the music business, but in this instance, it is 100 percent accurate. Ryan, Melody, Gregory, Deondra, and Desirae Brown—The 5 Browns—have truly become classical music's first family of piano virtuosos.

How did all this happen for them?

It was the mid-1990s. I was a top executive at Sony Music and producing gold and platinum records for artists such as Engelbert Humperdinck, Gloria Gaynor, Eddy Arnold, David Hasselhoff, Helen Reddy, and others. I had achieved platinum status selling two million CDs in the United Kingdom with eleven-year-old singing sensation Kaci, and I'd sold another million with fourteen-year-old Katie Cassidy (yes, David's daughter). Later I would score triple-platinum success with Jay-Z's *Black Album*, but for now all I wanted to do was jump on the boy-band gravy train and put together my own pop group, something along the lines of an 'N Sync or a Backstreet Boys.

It was August 23, 1998, 11 p.m. Exhausted after being in the studio all day mixing a new recording, and having just kissed my six-year-old daughter Briana good night, I sat on my couch brainlessly channel-surfing. On PBS, something jolted me out of my stupor and made me press "freeze frame" on the remote—there on the TV was a freckle-faced boy, about ten years old, light reddish-brown helmet hair, playing the keyboards with a flair and expertise I had never seen before. I watched on and learned that he was a winner in the youngest division of an elite international piano competition. PBS had arranged to film him and the other winners playing for their peers at an elementary school.

The four or five young performers who followed him were also amazing, but this redhead kid had the star quality that none of the others had. He was all-American. With his unassuming and relaxed demeanor, he looked like he had just stepped off a Little League diamond and onto the concert stage. His effusive personality also blew me away during an interview that followed his performance. It was uncanny that I had just said to a friend at lunch the day before how there was such a void for a boys' group with a new twist: talent being the centerpiece! What a treat it would be to work with truly gifted young people, rather than auto-tuning (bringing notes into pitch with a computer) a studio performance with some Milli Vanilli act, then having to generate enough promotion and press to hype the project up the charts to number one.

The next morning I woke up at five-thirty as usual, resolved to find that kid and make him the jumping-off point for the new and talented boy band I was about to create. Now came the first challenge—the only clue I had to find him had flashed across the bottom of the TV screen during his performance: "Ryan Brown, Alpine, Utah." I started by calling the national PBS headquarters, then PBS's Utah station. I got the same answer after speaking to countless people: "I have no idea who he is or how to find him." So I dug into the bag of tricks I had learned from selling life insurance long before I made my first music deal. After "googling" Alpine, Utah, to find out where the heck it was, I found the entire white pages for the city online and printed them out. "Here we go," I said to myself, and I began my quest to call every Brown family there, determined not to stop until I hit pay dirt.

Blurry-eyed and bordering on carpal-tunnel syndrome from punching the phone numbers of all the "A. Brown(s)," I started to pray that the father's name wasn't Zigfried. Persevering, I landed on and spoke to Brent Brown, who happened to be the uncle of Ryan and brother of Keith.

Bingo! After explaining to him that I was a record producer and had seen Ryan on TV, I asked how I could reach the boy's parents about an idea I had. He informed me that Ryan and his family no longer lived in Utah but had moved to New York, where young Ryan was attending Juilliard. Since Brent was rushing out the door, our conversation was brief, but I got what I needed: *the golden phone number.*

Within seconds I started dialing Keith when it dawned on me how Brent had so casually mentioned that Ryan was attending Juilliard; now that, as they say in Yiddish, is bashert (meant to be). I had lived in New York City for twenty-two years and had learned most facets of the music business quite well under the tutelage of Clive Davis, who appointed me to his elite artists and repertoire (A&R) team and gave me the double duty of heading up CBS/Sony Music Publishing. However, I had very little knowledge, if any, of the classical music world. The only thing I did know was that Juilliard is the country's most elite music conservatory and harder to get into than Harvard; each freshman class of musicians, actors, and dancers consists of only eighty students. Pianists from all over the world apply, and only five percent—the crème de la crème—get accepted.

Now I anticipated, getting ready to speak to Keith Brown, that he might be a classical stuffed shirt and imply that his child was superior to the banal world of pop music, so before he picked up the phone I had to decide how I'd open the conversation and sell him on my vision of Ryan as the next Justin Timberlake. I knew that in this case I had to rely on my favorite Albert Einstein quote, *"Imagination is more important than knowledge."* When Keith picked up, I could hardly hear his voice, which was being drowned out by the clamor of what sounded like fifty pianos playing at the same time on his end of the phone. My first thought was that he must be in a piano store with Ryan. He apologized for the "noise" and said he would step into his garage where it was a bit quieter. His voice could not have been more pleasant—

receptive and friendly. Now the moment of truth had arrived. I had learned years before from my dad that there is no second chance for a first impression. I knew I had only one shot to convince him that I'd make his son rich and famous and have all the little girls running after him. I had no clue at the time how truly unimportant and insignificant these things are within the Mormon community.

Keith, who I found out later is one of the kindest and most respectful people I have ever met, would never have tried to patronize me for not knowing classical music or Mormon values. Instead, he methodically explained to me that the international piano competition and the PBS show I had seen had taken place three years earlier and had been recycled as reruns several times since its original airing. He declined my fame-and-fortune pitch and told me that Ryan, now thirteen years old and attending Juilliard's Pre-College program, was pretty much focused on classical music, his education, and his lessons and was studying with famed Juilliard professor Yoheved Kaplinsky.

Then in one sentence, uttered offhandedly and without any hint of portent, Keith Brown would not only change the lives of all his children but also the landscape of classical music itself. He said, "*I don't know if you're interested or not, but there are four more at home like that.*"

Double Bingo! My creative juices went into overdrive. Did I just hear that right? Did he just tell me that he had five children of equal talent who were all at the famed school at the same time? After a long pause on my end and time to recover from his statement, I asked him to elaborate. His two eldest, Desirae and Deondra, had auditioned with hundreds of hopefuls worldwide, vying for just seventeen piano positions at Juilliard's college division, and both were accepted to pursue bachelor's degrees. The following year, the three younger siblings auditioned with hundreds of other young pianists to gain entrance into the Pre-College division, where they would study with the same teachers as their older sisters, and they too were admitted. All five had received full or nearly full scholarships—the family could never have managed the $30,000 per year tuition for each son and daughter. The entire family packed up their five grand pianos and headed east to New York City; there was no way that Ryan's parents, Keith and Lisa Brown, could remain in the heart of the Rocky Mountains when each of their five children was about to embark on such a life-changing experience.

I was now embarrassed for even suggesting that Ryan join my *boy band*. The Brown kids' accomplishments at Juilliard had no parallel—Ryan, Melody, Gregory, Deondra, and Desirae were the first and only five siblings ever to attend Juilliard at the same time in the school's 100-year history. Now that, I thought, is a publicist's dream. My phone conversation with Keith ended with the understanding that nothing should distract the kids from their education, and for the time being we would put the entire conversation in mothballs. We traded contact information, and I told him that I would stay in touch.

And stay in touch I did. Over the next four years, although we still had never met, I was diligent in communicating with Keith Brown on a regular basis. The kids rose through the degree programs at Juilliard, re-auditioning each step of the way, from Pre-College to the undergraduate program and on to their master's degrees. There are no special treatments or gimmicks of any kind at Juilliard for auditions and acceptance, just hard work and tons of talent.

The Brown family phenomenon would not stay a secret confined to Juilliard for too much longer, though. The genie finally escaped from the bottle when the kids' story leaked out and caught the attention of the media, including the BBC in England, which ran a TV piece emceed by Geri Halliwell, aka Ginger Spice of the Spice Girls. This piqued *The New York Times*, which in turn enticed *60 Minutes* to run a story that to date has aired five times—an unprecedented run for the TV show. Shortly thereafter, *People* magazine referred to the kids as the "Fab Five," and Oprah called them "the chosen few." But nobody from the stodgy, unimaginative music industry ever picked up on this musical marvel. Juilliard even had professors on staff to help soloists with their careers, but when it came to *five soloists in one*, the professors were stuck.

In 2003 Keith invited me to the graduation of his two eldest, Desirae and Deondra. I would finally meet Keith and the entire family and, as they say in the business, see if we would vibe together. We met at the exclusive Phillips Club (literally ten steps across the street from Juilliard) for our first meeting and think-tank session. It took me a little while to get into my rhythm, as I had always worked with pop, rock, or R&B groups and this was uncharted territory for me. That being said, after some warm-up conversation I finally asked the five prodigies the key question: "In a perfect world, what is your ultimate goal?" It was obvious to them but not to me. "All we want to do," they answered without missing a beat, "is to pool our talent, perform together, and inspire kids our age with the message that classical music could be cool if it had a new makeover."

The meeting turned out to be over-the-top great, and in my next phone call to Keith, he gave me the green light. "Go knock yourself out and see what you come up with," he said, surely thinking not much would happen. Although the music business had taught me the hard lesson to *always get a signed piece of paper*, I sealed this contractual agreement as personal manager and executive producer for the Brown family with a mere *phone shake*, and that was it. This good-faith, no-pressure agreement, I found out later, had earned me their trust and was a major factor in Keith allowing me the privilege of representing his kids.

The old adage, "Be careful what you wish for because you may just get it," was now truer than ever for me. I needed the kids to audition for prospective record labels, agents, and publicists—but how in the world would I ever get five concert pianos into one room? While heading the music publishing company Mercury Records in the mid-'80s, I remembered, I would walk by Steinway Hall on West 57th Street almost daily, never giving it a second thought and certainly never having any interest to walk in. "Okay," I thought, "in the worst-case scenario, all they could do was laugh at me for even suggesting the idea of setting up five concert pianos in one room." After all, I lived by the proverb that great ideas pass through three stages: first they are ridiculed, then they are violently opposed, and then they are accepted as self-evident.

Within a few weeks, on one of my scheduled trips to New York from my home in L.A., I walked into Steinway Hall for the first time and asked the receptionist if I might speak to someone about leasing one of their music rooms for two days. I was referred to Ms. Irene Wlodarski. Sheepishly and hoping that she would not think I was completely nuts, I asked Ms. Wlodarski, "Do you think there is some way I could lease out one of your music rooms for two days with five Steinway concert pianos already set up?" The answer was a surprisingly quick "Yes, of course." One major stumbling block down and one to go.

Being a neophyte in the world of classical music, I had no names or contacts to call—not unlike how I had *started* in the music business, when all I had were the yellow pages, a fistful of dimes, and a comfy indoor phone booth at the Americana Hotel. But after thirty years, the playing field had changed for me, and I had solid relationships with the CEOs and presidents of many top labels. I had given David Geffen one of his first seven-figure deals for writer and singer Laura Nyro; I had given Tommy Mottola his first job in the business as my assistant, and he went on to become the longest-running president of Sony Music Entertainment and husband to Mariah Carey; there was also Doug Morris, whom

I used to pitch songs to when he was owner of Big Tree Records. I decided to contact all the people I knew at the top, and they would put me in touch with the heads of the classical music divisions at their labels. I used the same resources to contact top brass at personal appearance agencies and PR firms as well.

Within weeks, and with the help of Keith and his wife, Lisa (who I found out is the heart and soul of the family), I staged and orchestrated a forty-five-minute showcase at Steinway Hall replete with five concert pianos in one room. We decided not to tell the kids that some of the biggest power players in the music industry *might* show up, as the five of them were under enough stress, but they instinctively knew that a lot was riding on their performance that day, and that they had to be on top of their game.

On the first day's showcase at Steinway Hall, at least three record company presidents attended, including Gilbert Hetherwick, with whom we ultimately signed, plus top-level executives from Sony, BMG, Atlantic, Universal Music, and other major labels. The following day there were top-level executives from major talent agencies and public relations firms, including ICM, William Morris, Columbia Artists, and Rogers & Cowan. It was one of those rare occasions when everybody who was invited actually showed up! Keith and I would introduce the family and preface the performance by saying that everybody in the room was about to see something they had never seen before. We'd explain to our elite audience how the music had been arranged especially for the five Brown kids to play on five pianos at the same time. We'd also explain that, to mix things up a little, we wouldn't have all five Browns play every piece together, as that would defeat the purpose of each one having been trained as a solo concert pianist. It was important that each of the five kids demonstrate his or her unique style and skills. It would also give the record labels more possibilities to ponder for a first CD.

Many people along the way have asked me my secret for creating stars, and I simply tell them, it happens when *preparation meets opportunity*. The Browns' showcase certainly reflected that secret. Although everybody in the room had a full schedule, not a single person left early to get to another appointment. Quite the contrary—these fierce competitors, much to my amusement, even mingled and stayed long after the showcase ended to talk to the five siblings, to Keith and Lisa, and to me. What they just experienced had truly amazed them.

In another stroke of serendipity, this was also the beginning of the Brown family's proud association with Steinway and their first step to becoming exclusive Steinway artists. Without Steinway providing the five matching concert grand pianos—altogether worth over half-a-million dollars—and Wheaton Van Lines to move them around, it would have been near impossible to go out on the road and perform.

On the plane back to L.A., I could not stop thinking how cool, calm, collected, and personable the Brown kids were; in fact, even I had never witnessed such a musical experience. When I got to my office the next morning, I knew we had captured lightning in a bottle—every person who had attended the showcase had left me either voice mail or e-mail; that just does not happen! They all expressed their enthusiasm and excitement for the kids, but even more important: "How soon can we sign them?"

We hit the lottery!

I called Keith and Lisa with the good news and told them that we had to strike while the iron was hot. The three of us returned to New York within days for back-to-back meetings, with scarcely enough space in between to breathe. It was critical for us to determine which company's vision was the same as ours, how much they were prepared to promote and market the Brown family, and equally important, their understanding and respect for the Browns' artistry and family values. We would need a top music business attorney to help us negotiate the deals once we made our decisions, so I also set up meetings with several powerhouse music business attorneys before leaving L.A.

We saw, we came, we conquered! After meeting with each company, there was a lot to digest and so much at stake. We could not afford one misstep, since we now had our choice of *the best of the best*. After careful deliberation we finally chose our dream team: BMG Masterworks for our record label; ICM for our concerts; Rogers & Cowan for publicity and PR; and Fred Davis, one of the most sought-after and respected music business attorneys (and son of Clive Davis) for legal counsel.

In one of our first meetings that included the kids, we emphasized to BMG Masterworks that our goal was to show all the children taking piano lessons, violin lessons, or performing in school orchestras, bands, or choirs that there was much more to classical music than geriatric concerts and stiff, tuxedo-clad musicians, which made the genre so unappealing to young people.

The Brown kids told everybody on the team that they intended to dress as they normally did, youthful and relaxed—no tux, no tails, no formal gowns. Although there was initial grumbling from some of the stalwart BMG executives, the Browns held firm to their core beliefs, explaining that they must stay true to themselves. They never wanted their nonconformity to be a gimmick; they simply wanted to project an image of five talented young pianists who also enjoyed sports, shopping (the girls, at least), movies, novels, video games, bowling, ping pong, and just hanging out together. They truly were best friends who happened to be siblings and who enjoyed performing together as well. This camaraderie expressed itself in their first CD photo shoot for BMG and press shots for Rogers & Cowan.

With all the excitement and decision-making, we forgot one last thing—*a name*! What would best describe

Ryan, Melody, Gregory, Deondra, and Desirae as a family? We spent hours bouncing names around, keeping in mind the importance of clearing a .com following whichever one we chose. After hours of running through exotic, neurotic, romantic, and serious names, we went back to basics and christened the five Browns—duh—"The 5 Browns," and I immediately locked up www.the5browns.com.

Next on the agenda was repertoire for The 5 Browns' first CD. Lisa was a major factor in working closely with Debbie Surdi, the head of A&R for BMG Masterworks, to accomplish this. The kids decided that shorter pieces should be chosen—three to eight minutes long—so that a younger audience, including classical newcomers, could best relate. Not wanting to alienate the core classical audience, however, they also included several interesting and obscure pieces that even a connoisseur could appreciate. Two arrangers, Jeffrey Shumway and Kendall Briggs, were assigned several familiar orchestra pieces that Lisa, a trained opera singer herself, and the kids chose. They had the various sections of the orchestra transcribed and implemented so that the parts and melody were evenly distributed among the five pianos. The arrangers were also required to make sure that all five parts be extremely challenging, equal in difficulty, and even virtuosic. To further develop and arrange music for five piano solos, duos, and trios, they recruited the skills of arrangers Greg Anderson and John Novacek as well.

In order to make the April 5, 2005, release date, the kids raced to learn each piece of music as soon as the arrangers completed them, and they juggled all this with their Juilliard commitments in the late spring semester of 2004. The last arrangement of the five piano pieces wasn't completed until July that year, and the recording sessions were set for August. To add even more pressure, all of the music needed to be memorized. This is certainly not the norm for studio sessions, but The 5 Browns knew that if they were to attain perfect ensemble and uniform dynamics in the studio, they would have to focus on one another rather than refer to musical notes sketched on staffs and bars in the handwritten score.

Their first recording session was line-produced by multiplatinum classical and Broadway producer Jay Sachs. The mutual respect between Jay and the kids coupled with their combined talent resulted in a magnificent first CD. Self-titled *The 5 Browns*, it shot clear to the number one debut spot in *Billboard* magazine and held there for a consecutive eight weeks, unseating classical superstar Yo-Yo Ma (whom the Browns have always revered) from his nineteen-week reign. The 5 Browns were off and running, with radio and TV appearances including *The Tonight Show* with Jay Leno, *Good Morning America*, *The View*, *The Martha Stewart Show*, a live outdoor performance on *The Today Show*, plus the additional reruns and updates on *60 Minutes*. Their print media blitz included *The New York Times*, *Parade*, the *Los Angeles Times*, *The Sunday Telegraph*, and *Reader's Digest*. Amazingly, the critics loved The 5 Browns almost as much as the public. Tom Manoff of NPR said on the air, "The 5 Browns exude a kind of freshness and energy once called 'All-American.'" *Entertainment Weekly* referred to them as "five young Mormons who all play scorching piano, thundering down on five Steinways together; they are button-down cute and yet somewhat worldly." After an appearance with the Dallas Symphony, the usually harsh *Dallas Morning News* critic was quoted as saying, "Send them out to schools from shore to shore, with piano teachers on hand to sign up students afterward, and the future of classical music will look a lot brighter."

With the meteoric success of *The 5 Browns*, BMG Masterworks—now Sony/BMG—was quick to release a second CD. Entitled *No Boundaries*, it again required the kids to rehearse and memorize all the material while attending classes at Juilliard, and now there was even one more element that had to be worked in—120 concert appearances across the country. With the first CD still going strong on the *Billboard* charts, *No Boundaries* also debuted at number one and held the spot for an unheard-of twenty-one straight weeks. For much of the time, The 5 Browns held both the number one and number two spots on the charts with their first and second CDs.

For CD number three, the Browns blended the beautiful, romantic elements of classical music with the sad notes found in jazz and blues. Peppered in were several collaborations, such as renowned jazz trumpeter Chris Botti playing *An American in Paris* with the five pianos and the world-famous violinist Gil Shaham playing with two pianos on "Aquarium" from *Carnival of the Animals*. Fittingly titled *Browns in Blue*, this CD also hit number one, making it *three for three* for The 5 Browns.

The group is now booked almost two years ahead of time, with few open dates. They have tapped a new audience and awakened classical music; according to Sandy Friedman, vice president of Rogers & Cowan, "The 5 Browns are doing for classical music what Tiger Woods has done for golf." During their concerts there are people *dancing in the aisles*, and in one packed concert hall in Arizona the roar of 2,500 screaming grade school and high school kids nearly swept the The 5 Browns off the stage. Then there were the deafening cheers of 4,000 kids in the college basketball arena in a small Idaho town, so packed that even the seats with virtually no view were occupied.

At this point we felt we needed more of an international presence. We changed agencies, leaving ICM and signing on to IMG Artists under the guiding hand of Elizabeth Sobol. She set up concerts in the United Kingdom, France, Germany, and Asia. Although the number of concert-goers under thirty years old was unprecedented at The 5 Browns' U.S. concerts, it was astronomical in Japan, where a typical audience of two to three thousand people was roughly forty percent under thirty, and it was unbelievable in

Korea, at probably fifty percent. Huge numbers of schoolkids taking piano lessons would come with their parents, and as young fans have always done in the U.S., they'd wait for up to an hour after a performance ended to meet The 5 Browns and get their autographs.

With the Chinese so devoted to classical piano music––over fifty million of their youngsters study formal piano—IMG is planning a mass media explosion in that country, perhaps of a magnitude never before seen there, that will include multiple concert tours and endorsements.

By all measures, The 5 Browns have delivered on their goal to change the face of classical music.

Over the past few years, The 5 Browns have journeyed down an almost providential path, demystifying the often-misunderstood genre of music we call classical, and they have already lived a lifetime of experiences. They have met countless young people who have been inspired by their music, and who in turn have inspired The 5 Browns with their touching stories.

I had arranged for my dear friends Julie Chrystyn and Dwight Opperman to see The 5 Browns perform in Phoenix. Once more by "grand design," Mr. O (as we call him) and Julie had just taken over a major publishing company called Phoenix Books. What a natural next step it was for me to talk to them about the idea of The 5 Browns telling their stories to the world; their response was extremely enthusiastic, and with the support and direction of another longtime acquaintance, Phoenix Books president and CEO Michael Viner, the book you are now reading came into being.

The 5 Browns' insights will relate to readers of all ages. They are found in this collection of true stories and vignettes, written by each one of the siblings in his or her own words. Take the journey with Ryan, Melody, Gregory, Deondra, and Desirae—laugh, cry, reflect—and enjoy listening to their concert on the enclosed CD while you read. As you listen you will have fun matching their individual styles of playing with their individual personalities. Get ready as The 5 Browns take their places at the pianos—their eyes lock—a silent signal passes between them, and in a mere instant they are transformed from regular kids into musical dynamos, flawless in precision and brimming with passion. They have shattered all the preconceptions of those who thought classical music must be inscrutable or intimidating. As the *New York Post* proclaimed, "*One family, five pianos, and fifty fingers add up to the biggest classical music sensation in years.*"

✳ ✳ ✳

*You have–one new voice message–left–today–at 12:38–p.m.:
"Yeah, hi, Greg, this is Doodle Bowen from the Office of Student Affairs.
I'm just calling to see if you could come in and see me in my office
sometime today. It's about the grad recital posters you've put up. Uh,
yeah...some members of the faculty have taken a bit of offense to them,
and they've requested they be removed. Give me a call back when you
can, or just knock on my door. Thanks."*

THE 5 WHO?

BY GREGORY BROWN

The Juilliard School
New York City
December 2005

So, for anyone out there who's not particularly
familiar with the ins and outs of top-tier music schools, one
might be tempted to assume that the entrance audition is the
toughest thing a student goes through in order to be assured
their degree. Well, that person would be, in many ways, dead
wrong. It becomes apparent very early on that it is much more
difficult to get *out* of the divine bubble than it is to get in.
Granted, students graduate from these classical institutions
every year, as I eventually did, but to get out unfazed, with
self-respect and perspective intact, is a rarity indeed.

Probably the most unsavory and universally traumatizing
of the requirements for graduating is the one for which you
receive next to no scholastic credit—this, of course, is the
infamous graduation recital. Again, one might wonder, "Now
wait, what's the big deal with that? Isn't playing the piano
what you love to do? How is that unsavory?" A valid
question, and if merely playing the piano was all that goes
into these recitals, I would be ashamed of myself for ever

using the words *piano* and *unsavory* in the same sentence. Luckily, such feelings of shame are nowhere to be found.

The graduation recital is an age-old initiation rite, preliminary to becoming one of the "chosen few." I can't help but recall images from a *National Geographic* special I once saw that documented an African tribe during the initiation of their sons into manhood. I'll refrain from elaborating on the unpleasant details, but let's just say I felt an odd kinship with those poor little buddies. The difference between us music students and those boys, however, was the slight trade off of physical pain and humiliation for mental pain and humiliation—which is much less criminal in a "civilized" society like our own. But then again, who wouldn't take a flogging to the jewels if the compensation were the honor of being called a man?

For a clearer picture, let's take a little walk through Juilliard, seek out some callow soul, pre-manhood, and follow him through his rite of passage. We can call our hypothetical little stooge Greg, for now.

Greg sits in a practice room, surrounded by paper-thin walls on all sides. He's trying to practice one of the pieces that he needs to have prepared for his looming recital, but he doesn't yet know it as well as the guy showing off next door to him. That guy's playing the same piece twice as fast, so either he's just better than Greg or he's had more time with the piece. Either way, there are no empty rooms to switch to, so Greg practices on masochistically in this lopsided duel. It's a lesson day, so he's got to take the piece to his teacher today too. His fellow students in the practice rooms, as well as one of the greatest teachers in the world, have now heard him fumble through the piece. She's not very happy with him, because he's got only two more weeks until his recital, and she has Pre-College students who are sounding better. She tells him he needs to practice a heck of a lot more if he plans on being ready in time. He says he will be, but he's just humoring her. He knows that the assignments of his other classes won't allow him that time. He does try, though, and ends up taking the time from dinner and from sleeping, but before he knows it, the day of his recital is upon him, and his music is still not solid. He tries to convince himself that it's just a school recital, and no one's ever prepared for these things. Everyone plays brand-new music that isn't fully solid, so they'll understand. But he knows that's not really true, because he's gone to the recitals of his fellow students and been present for the lashing they've gotten behind their backs in cafeteria and practice-room conversations. "Isn't he supposed to be good?" "I can't believe he won that competition last year." "He couldn't even get through his Beethoven." "It's so unfair that he's got a job."

Greg knew what was coming, but he really wanted to be called a man, even if it was at the expense of his self-respect. So he walks out onstage. Bowing, he peers out into the audience and notices some friendly faces—people who came to hear him because they love him and love music. But then he glances two rows back, and reality sets in. Probably two thirds of the people sitting before him have not come out of love for him or for music. He sits down and begins to play. His heart is in his throat, so he starts to rush the tempo and loses control. He stumbles on a passage and tries to cover it by jumping to the recap. The unfriendly faces flash through his mind, as he scolds himself for giving them the satisfaction of hearing him fall apart. Now flustered and without an ounce of confidence, Greg plays on, praying with every note that it will soon be over. Finally he walks offstage, feeling about as big as his pinky finger, and it hits him that this was never meant to be a music concert at all. It is, and always was, merely an occasion to stand for an hour in front of the class in nothing but his underwear. But the passage into manhood is universal, and the unfriendly faces in the back will have their tighty-whiteys exposed in due course before they too can become respectable in the divine bubble we know as the world of *classical music*.

Okay, so I'll let you in on a little secret. Our hypothetical stooge, Greg? You guessed it—yours truly. As I was preparing for this public spectacle, the dread of it all was becoming unbearable, so I decided to take it for what it was and have a little fun with the situation. What lowly college student doesn't want to stick it to the man every once in a while by having a little fun? So, naturally, my scheming began.

You see, by the time of this recital, my siblings and I had already been The 5 Browns for about a year and a half. The success of our first CD caught a lot of people (including us) by surprise, and the incredible media attention and performance opportunities that resulted are insanely rare for classical musicians. Needless to say, we felt blessed—almost unfairly—by everything that was happening so early in our careers, and that considered, it was kind of an unspoken rule that we wouldn't talk about these things at school. We acted like The 5 Browns didn't exist, the school acted like The 5 Browns didn't exist, and the students (aside from a few close friends) acted like The 5 Browns didn't exist. We felt that there were so many talented kids at the school who deserved opportunities like ours, and we didn't want to seem boastful about our lucky breaks. The school ignored us because we presented classical music in a way that is the absolute opposite of how it has been done for the past seventy-five years. It became clear that we simply didn't see eye to eye with them, and that they didn't agree with or respect our efforts to shake things up and break down old barriers between the bubble and everyone else.

It wasn't just the school, either. Since we became an ensemble, it has taken us considerable effort to prove to the divine bubble as a whole that we're for real, that we can really play, and that we're every bit as passionate about our mission of bringing classical music to the masses as we say we are. The bubble itself knows that its days are numbered— it's obvious to most people within it—so many of its residents are gradually being convinced by our efforts. Then again, there are the old stalwarts who refuse to step out of the "good ole days" and into reality. Their ranks, however, are quickly thinning, and these "good ole days" will soon end up where they belong—in the past.

So to have a little fun with these stalwarts (who take things way too seriously), I figured I'd make a statement with my recital, and I'd do it through my posters. Every recital given at Juilliard has some sort of poster on the bulletin board to let the whole school know whose undies they get to see next. There are two different types of posters. The first, and most common, is the generic poster for either A) generic people, or B) people who want their "coming out parties" to fly under the radar. This school-issued poster just lists the name of the performer and the names of the pieces being played. The second type of poster is the homemade version. This can be anything that you want it to be, so long as it's approved by the Office of Student Affairs. You post these flyers if you A) want to show everyone how stunning you look in your new headshot, B) want your recital poster to stand out from the crowd because you beat the odds and want people to be impressed that you're actually prepared, or C) want to use humor as a defense mechanism so that people laugh so hard they forget there's even a recital at all. I, of course, opted for C.

After a lot of thought, I decided that the funniest and most appropriate way to go about this would be to make fun of myself along with a few people who represent the classical establishment. I added myself into the mix so that it would be clear that it was all done in good fun. A really good place to start would be the picture that oh-so-glamorously graced the cover or our first CD. It was obvious that this wasn't a 5 Browns concert, so I couldn't well have my siblings displayed on my own grad-recital poster. That would just look like I was trying to show off the fact that we had a record deal, which would be so incredibly lame that I'd be forced to kick my own butt. So, using my trusty Photoshop as a scalpel, I surgically removed each one of my siblings' cute little smiling faces, one by one, until I was left with an intact Greg Brown and four gracefully posed yet noggin-less bodies. Now is where the fun starts. What should I put in place of their heads? Thank you, Google Images! Instantly, I had access to every picture posted online of any Juilliard faculty member or administrator I could think of. Jackpot! After singling out the funniest photos of my favorite teachers and other notorious Juilliard brass, I saw that I had way more than four. I couldn't possibly let these precious treasures go to waste, so I would simply have to make more than one version of the poster.

After a few hours of touchup—time well spent, considering the losing battle I otherwise would have been fighting in some practice room—the surgery was at last complete. Suddenly, the coolest seventy-five-year-old woman at Juilliard had the body of a bony twenty-year-old boy, and one of my favorite teachers (a masculine old man who looks something like Dracula) now donned a stylish little black top with cap sleeves to complement the handsome Bohemian necklace around his now delicate neck. As I sat alone in my apartment bedroom, staring at the beauty I had just created with my own two hands, I couldn't help but shed a few tears of painful laughter. There they were, eight of the most identifiable people at Juilliard, all posing with me in the oddest faux-album-cover of all time. Needless to say, I was quite proud of my work.

I couldn't end there, though. There had to be something more that I could do with these posters, but how can you make faculty heads on your siblings' bodies any funnier? Obviously, there was only one viable answer here— absurd, fabricated quotes! It's an exhilarating feeling, having empty comic bubbles hovering over the superimposed heads of your most well known superiors, and having the power to fill them in with whatever you choose. You can make them say such kind things—"Greg Brown is like the son I never had" or "Greg Brown is the next Bette Midler." Or, if so compelled, you can make them say much more realistic things—"I like fuzzy bunnies," or my personal favorite, "the 5 who?"

After taking great care to make sure each person (including me) was saying something utterly ridiculous, I knew my job was nearly complete. There was just one more thing for me to do—further make fun of myself. If I gave myself the worst of it, how could anyone else possibly get upset? It seemed like a fail-safe plan, so I went to work on a third poster, which would use only my head on each body. You know, I had never considered until that moment just how stunning I would look as a girl. I must say, the chic outfits and feminine poses complemented my manly sideburns quite nicely.

The three works of art in hand (which did, incidentally, include the date and time of the recital in fine print near the bottom), I went to get them approved. This posed the only conceivable hurdle. I went into the office and handed my posters to the lady. She looked at them for a few long seconds, which made me nervous, but once she started to chuckle I knew I had succeeded. She stamped each one, handed them back to me, and I went to hang them on the school poster boards. I also decided to put copies of all three on my locker, as it was both a highly trafficked area by students and a place that faculty members rarely wandered. All day, that first day, I had people coming up to me, telling me they had never seen anything so funny in their lives, and praising me for my courage. The next morning, however, I got to school to find that the posters were all gone. My first thought was that they had probably been taken by students who thought they were funny, but after replacing them, they had disappeared again by the following morning. Something was up. This continued for several days until the afternoon before my recital, when I finally received the phone call I had been expecting from the Office of Student Affairs.

"Yeah, hi, Greg, this is Doodle Bowen from the Office of Student Affairs. I'm just calling to see if you could come in and see me in my office sometime today. It's about the grad recital posters you've put up. Uh, yeah...some members of the faculty have taken a bit of offense to them, and they've requested they be removed. Give me a call back when you can, or just knock on my door. Thanks."

"Figures!" was my first thought. I had totally seen this coming. There are always going to be people who take their lives way too seriously and get up in arms over the dumbest things. I didn't really feel like going into Doodle's office, so I called him back instead.

"Yeah, I know we stamped your posters, but I got a call from Irma Prince the other day, and she wasn't really very happy about her face being used. Now, I can't *make* you do anything, but I think it would be a good idea to send her an e-mail of apology or something. It's up to you, though. As far as the posters are concerned, I'm gonna have to ask you to stop putting up more stamped ones."

That was no problem. The recital was in a day, and I didn't actually want people to come anyway. It was this "e-mail of apology" that irked me. Ms. Prince was the only "head" that I didn't know personally. I had cast her in my poster because her "distinct" personality made the motley crew of mismatched characters so much funnier, and I couldn't resist. I did, however, go much easier on her than I had with some of the others. First, I put her head on the body of one of my sisters, so at least her gender was right, and second, her quote was pretty benign. I've tried turning the tables and putting myself in her position. For instance, if she were to make my head say "Irma Prince is my skinny little teddy bear, and I'm her schnookie wookums," would I demand that *her* posters be ripped down? I guess rhetorical questions like this need no answer.

Even though I was ticked off by her reaction and the fact that it had caused my hard work to be vandalized night after night, I knew that if I had offended her somehow, I should try to apologize. I got her e-mail address and went to work. It was probably wrong to use her image without asking her first, so I told her there was no excuse for that. However, that being said, if the posters were truly beyond the line of acceptability, as she claimed they were, then the Office of Student Affairs should never have approved them in the first place, and she should take it up with them. Plus, the reactions I'd heard from other faculty members whose likenesses I had used were quite a bit different from her own. I was subtle and polite about it, but honestly, immature morons like me are exactly why they have an approval process like this. I never heard back from her, but she did say "hi" to me at graduation, so maybe I've still got a chance to be her skinny little teddy bear after all.

After a day or two of feeling satisfied by my irreverence with the posters, I suddenly found that this feeling was being taken over by a sincere sadness. Why did I have to feel guilty for not treating myself, and classical music, as solemnly as the respected told me I should? Although the whole episode was kind of silly, it was about more than a few superimposed heads. It was another manifestation of the conflict my siblings and I had begun to know so well. Was it so wrong to want to step out of the bubble and be myself? Why was I required to conform to stale, enormously ostracizing tradition? How long was I going to have to clash with those who believe that you have to hoard what you love in order to keep it sacred?

The fact that I am continually forced to ask myself these questions, even now, proves to me that the divine bubble of high musical art—the *renowned* conservatories, the *elite* institutions, the *important* connoisseurs—are missing the point. I go out onstage every night because I have *fun* doing it. I love this music more than almost anything! I love helping new people fall in love with it. I love watching the faces of little kids light up when we play "Flight of the Bumblebee." I love going to small blue-collar towns and introducing this great art to people who have never had the opportunity to experience it. I love proving to these people that you don't have to understand the structural intricacies of the form in order to be inspired and moved by the power within this music. This is all *fun* for me. These old stalwarts——when is the last time they went to a concert in order to feel like a kid again? I guess they just don't quite understand what they're missing. Yes, Beethoven and Bach were serious composers, and yes, their music is great, but who's to say that exalting it is more satisfying than loosening your tie and enjoying it? Respect is overrated. Why should I care about the validation and respect of a bubble, which I am doing my utmost to burst? I see now that I no longer care to be called a man. The men of this world have forgotten how to have fun with what they cherish.

The stalwarts merely see five punks who are trying to destroy the treasures they hoard, but all we see is beauty being hidden, inspiration being blocked, our favorite amusement park becoming an empty museum, relevance lost in a shrine to irrelevance. This dying breed of curators can tear down our nonconformist posters all they want, but we'll simply put them right back up. It's just way too much fun when they're up there, for the world to see.

* * *

"If someone were to ask me what I did in my nine years in New York City, I would say I spent eight of them in a fifteen-foot-by-fifteen-foot blue-velvet-curtained room—the practice room."

RAZOR BLADES BETWEEN THE KEYS

BY MELODY BROWN

The Juilliard School
1997–2006

To tell you the truth, I was scared. The practice room was where all the rumors started, and here I was sitting in it, at an allegedly sabotaged piano. In two hours I would be auditioning for one of the top music schools in the country. I was paralyzed.

Voices floated through my head: "I've heard people stick razor blades between the keys." "It's a school full of backstabbers." "You'll never be the best." "If you don't learn and memorize a new work of music every week then you get kicked out." And yet above all was the voice that really paralyzed me: "You'll never get in anyway."

First of all, *were* there razor blades between the keys? Rumor had it that the school was so competitive that people hid razor blades in the cracks of the keys of practice pianos. I knew it had to be a myth, though I checked my keys anyway.

I was thirteen. My older sisters, Desirae and Deondra, had been at Juilliard for a year. They wanted Gregory, Ryan, and me to audition for the Pre-College division, where talented underage musicians get to learn from many of the same prestigious faculty. My sisters figured that a chance to study with these world-class teachers would be worth the move to New York.

Gregory, Ryan, and I didn't quite know how to feel about this. Juilliard was a scary thought. And yet we were curious, being driven by something so much stronger: pain. Practicing such long hours for competitions and concerts hurt. "No pain, no gain" seemed to be our motto. It was so bad that there were days where we couldn't play at all. And now we were hearing from our sisters that there was help. Pain evidently didn't have to be our only option.

Even though we hoped the Pre-College was our answer, I couldn't help but be frightened. Was I ready to be at a place like this? Hearing the pianist in the practice room next door to mine was like hearing Horowitz play. In the midst of the most talented, could I even survive if I miraculously got in?

I knew I needed to stop thinking and start practicing. I had two hours before my fate was decided. In the middle of practicing my Chopin, I happened to look up at something faintly etched into the black paint of the door. Straining my eyes to see what someone had carved, I finally made out the words "Pre-College Sucks."

This marked the beginning of my relationship with the school practice rooms. Initially the rumors like those above instilled fear, but later on they produced only laughter. I did happen, miraculously, to be accepted, and in so doing, the secrets of such a rumored school would finally be exposed. The practice room was where it all started.

Although I can honestly say that I never found any razor blades between the keys, I did find…well, other things in my new home. Here is a testament to what the "practice room" really is.

First of all, it *was* home. If someone were to ask me what I did in my nine years in New York City, I would say I spent eight of them in a fifteen-foot-by-fifteen-foot blue-velvet-curtained room. You would probably expect to hear something like "we did everything but eat and sleep in there," but that would be a lie. We did *everything* in there, including eating and sleeping.

Although each room had a very visible sign saying "No food or drink," how could one obey such a rule when people *lived* in there? Being any sort of music performance major meant you needed to live there. We were all constantly cramming. There were lessons, competitions, performing classes, theory classes, rehearsals, recitals, coachings, and finally the annual juries where you played in front of the legendary faculty to be graded. If you didn't live in there, you wouldn't be able to keep up. Food and drink found their way into the rooms.

On the outside it would appear harmless, but food could be used as a weapon. I admit I'm guilty of using it as such. Here's how.

There are times of desperation, where getting an hour of practice in before a two-hour class won't cut it. The class ends, leaving you with up to an hour to waste looking for another room. So what do you do? You try and save the room. Two hours is a long time to stake claim to such a priceless commodity. I'd say it was possible, if only the light didn't go out.

You see, in every room you'll find a motion-sensor light. If it's working correctly, you have fifteen minutes to leave your room before it turns off automatically. If you fail to return, desperate searchers will come and take your room. These are the rules; a dark room means a surrendered room.

Victory can be called when the victor steps in to claim it. Yet the battle is not over. The nonexistent defender had a plan all along. The first hidden weapon is endless amounts of "things." There are umbrellas, stacks of music, papers, trash, homework, schoolbooks, hats, coats, sweaters, concert programs, calendars, mail, socks, gloves, scarves, and anything you would find in a school bag or locker. The "things" only deter the victor as he steps farther into the room. And yet the weapon of mass destruction has not been unleashed. Only when the person closes the door does it take hold. The nose surrenders first, then the mind. For the smell of extremely potent food is too much for the victor to handle. He tries to practice, but the reek of it makes him gag. Finally, breathing fresh air in the hall seems more sane than gagging through Beethoven. The absent defense wins.

I have to admit I never unleashed putrid weapons of mass destruction, though I did use soggy old sandwiches to help visually deter my foes.

One day I would be the defense, and the next I would be the victor. Searching for a room was frustrating. Walking the hallways for hours was torture. You saw everything while looking for a vacant room: people eating, chatting with friends, sleeping, picking their noses, or practicing their hearts out. Sometimes you saw nothing but a Rite-Aid ad staring back at you. This was the most exasperating of all: blocked windows.

Covering up the windows was a no-no. The security guards would even get you on that one. For years I couldn't understand why people did this—until I started doing it myself.

There were times where I'd be practicing innocently when something at the window caught my eye. Peripherally I would see people watching for minutes at a time. Mostly they were friends waiting for me to break, though others were competitive listeners. Over time I became incredibly paranoid of these listeners. I couldn't practice while thinking people were judging me. Blocking the window seemed to block the fear.

If I was on the other side of the door, however, things changed. I would always try to peak around the Rite-Aid ad to see what someone was attempting to cover up. Most of the time there was no one in there (saving a room no doubt), but once in a while you did see things you shouldn't. For instance, we found our closest friend making out with a guy she was secretly dating behind a not-so-covered window. My brother was shocked when he realized that the hair, hand, and lips he could see belonged to her. We felt bad when we finally had to confess; the ads never could completely cover the windows.

Romances were always one of the most difficult things to cover up, since so many started in the exposed practice rooms. Although I never experienced the thrill of a practice-room romance, somehow my name was engraved on one of the pianos as having had such. I don't know whether to feel honored or embarrassed at having my name eternally carved into a piano. The quote isn't very accurate to have as a permanent memento: "Melody, come back and kiss me—Ori."

First of all, Ori was one of our best friends in the Pre-College. Girls were and would always be only friends to him, never romantic interests. Thus he wouldn't have written that, and I know I didn't, so who did?

The mystery continued when we found another carving on that same piano. This one was difficultly engraved into one of the keys. It read, "Helen loves Greg Brown." Someone was an impostor. For I knew Gregory didn't write that, and our friend Helen would never have done so. Although they did end up dating, Gregory pursuing her, neither one was the type to do this. Plus the "Ori" quote was wrong, anyway; it was apparent that the perpetrator watched enough, but didn't know us very well.

Later, we found yet another carving. This was a different piano, but again the engraving was done into a key, setting a trend. It read "H.C. + G.B." I sometimes wonder what other students think when they practice on keys that talk about the supposed love life of my brother. For us it became a sort of landmark. All I would have to say was, "Oh, I'm in the carved G.B. room by the bathroom," and people would automatically know where I was.

Not only did we know the carvings or discreet writings of each of the rooms, we knew the sounds and timbre as well. Again, I could tell a friend to meet me in my practice room by describing it as "the loud, echo-y one," and once more they could find me. There were rooms that were too wet in sound, and those that were too dry. Some had blue velvet curtains on every wall to muffle the sound, where others had none. If I happened to be practicing *next* to the "loud, echo-y" room, I was in for an absolutely horrible day. If a trombone player happened to occupy this room, it got so loud and frustrating that I would rather brave the hallways than listen to his recital. If I chose to fight it, I would have to suffer through a mixture of my intimate Mozart and his blaring Wagner, and most of the time it just wasn't worth it.

When I would move on to a new room, I felt relieved to practice in peace. How could I know that the person next to me was only on a break? Ten minutes of solitude would pass when my poor Mozart started booming with Wagner again.

This happened constantly. Sometimes I would just end up sitting in the hallway, hopefully with a friend. Where two were, more would gather. Before you knew it, ten friends would be sitting in the hallway laughing and joking. If a room happened to be vacated, one would run to nab it and the party would move into the practice room. We'd mess around on the piano, playing the Beatles or Coldplay, singing, gossiping, venting, and ultimately not practicing. More would join the party. They'd bring their food, drinks, and drama. We didn't care if the carpet was dirty; we were sprawled all over, resting our chronically aching backs, necks, and arms.

These were the times when we relaxed. There was so much cramming and intensity that we needed to take an evening off when we were "technically" practicing. "Technically" meant we were at the practice facility. We could've taken the party out on the town, but then that would be slacking. For all intents and purposes, we *meant* to practice. There just weren't any rooms. And so memories were made. I can't remember the dozens of practice hours spent in the rooms, but I do remember and value these evenings more than just about anything else in those nine years.

I might have been relieved when I permanently stepped out of Juilliard wearing a graduation gown. But looking back on the room with blue velvet curtains, I see a home. It's a home of potent smells and lingering tastes, of sharing my favorite Chinese takeout or attempting to consume dry daily sandwiches. It was a place that even provided a carpet bed under the piano; the room tucking me in by turning off the lights after fifteen minutes. I would change my clothes for recitals, fix my hair, and put on makeup. I'd do homework, compose music, and conduct rhythmic assignments to myself. I'd talk to my parents or boys on the phone. I'd visit with friends and argue with enemies. I'd cry my eyes out, throw music across the room, and bang on the piano. I'd laugh until I couldn't breathe and play until I transcended the room.

This was what I found in the practice rooms. Razor blades were the least of my worries. For life was between those keys, nothing else.

* * *

Our concert touring has taken us to almost every state in the country, Europe, Asia, and South America. Sometimes we are reminded that the way we grew up isn't the way everybody else grew up. In fact, every once in a while, this realization kind of smacks us upside the head. We may think, with a half-smile, that we aren't in Kansas anymore. Then we realize, smiles dropping, that we're very, very far from Kansas....

FIVE BROWNS
AND A BLACK

BY DESIRAE BROWN

Somewhere in the Deep South
Spring 2006

Our drive into Oldtown, a city in the Deep South, was a silent one. We were all tired from our four-hour trip, and at this point in the tour, our SUV was littered with potato chips, fashion magazines, and stinky, shoeless feet. I think my brothers economize luggage space by cutting back on their sock usage. We had been getting on each other's nerves this particular trip and after a series of disagreements fell into drowsy silence. We finally started to roll into the "downtown" area of Oldtown. Even in small towns we liked to refer to the most populated or built-up part of town in this way. The "downtown" was always the fanciest part of town; but canned cut-beans sport the fancy label too.

So we were moving through the fancy part of town when one of us absentmindedly mentions to the window that it was kind of weird that there were three shacks next to that mansion.

"Yeah, that is kinda weird." More silence.

We passed a little trailer park that was separated from a grand plantation-style home by a low chain-link fence. We'd

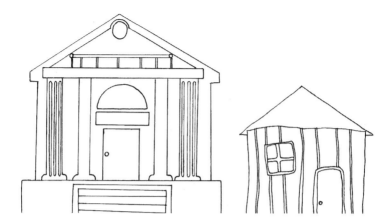

been to a lot of small towns, and this was not fitting the formula. Usually trailer parks were in one area of town, and grand plantation-style homes in another. We were confused. Since we had all lived many years in New York City, we thought ourselves decently versed in urban life. But real small-town life entranced us, and we observed this life with the fascination of little amateur scientists. We grew up in quite the small town of Alpine, Utah, but were only a thirty-minute drive from Salt Lake City. Because of this, we thought that maybe Alpine didn't truly count as a genuine small town. But Oldtown…now this was genuine.

Now we were all sitting up in our seats, staring out the windows: "Hey—do you guys see that huge cross in that front yard?"

"These people over here have got *more* than one cross in their yard."

"People still do that? What do you do with a big creepy cross in your yard? I mean what century are we in anyway?"

Old textbook pictures of the 1930s flashed through my mind of big, life-sized crosses in people's yards.

"Heeeyy…," I started slowly, "Does that gas station say what I think it does? Is the actual *name* of that gas station a racially derogatory term?" Everybody looked.

"What the—!"

"Are you kidding me...?"

"It's like we're in the Twilight Zone or something...."

"And dude, that guy's got a Confederate flag on the back of his truck!"

We all turned to look. Sure enough, a full-on flag was draped over the door to the flatbed and attached securely to show his southern pride. Another car sped past us with a smaller version of the flag displayed in his rear window.

"Don't people know that to most of the country a Confederate flag symbolizes slavery?" I asked. "And that it's a little bit offensive?"

We were totally feeling that we wanted to get out of the Deep South right then. But no, things were just beginning.

Our first stop was at a high school in town that had a music program. We usually offer to perform and speak in Arts Outreach programs wherever we go. We love it when kids get excited about music, and reaching out to them is probably one of the most important things we could do. On this particular day, as we were nearing the high school, we stopped gawking out the windows and started trying to "freshen" up. This involved crawling under and reaching over one another for the other black patent pump that slid under the seat, the vest in the bag underneath two other bags, and me once again asking Melody if I could borrow the powder in her bag.

We rushed into the high school—we rarely arrive at an event more than five minutes early—and started to do our thing. "Our thing" consists of playing the piano a little for the students, talking about the music, and then taking questions from them. On this occasion everything seemed to go fine. Nothing out of the ordinary. We began to think we might have been overreacting on our drive into town. Maybe the people here were totally normal? We finished up with the music students and made our way back to the car. We all assumed our might-as-well-be assigned seating as we waited for an escort to show us the way to the concert hall for our soundcheck.

Sitting there, I noticed something strange happening at the front of the school. Well, something *I*, the amateur little social scientist, had never seen before anyway. Classes had just ended, and as the students were coming out of school, I noticed that all the black football players and cheerleaders congregated on the far right side of the campus, while all the white football players and cheerleaders grouped on the left side. What was this...? I started looking around at the students in the fields and the sidewalks and the lawns, and the same thing was going on. It was like somebody had quickly sorted everything by color. Like we were in the 1930s or something.

I turned to my husband, Bryan, who had met up with us on this tour, and asked, "You notice anything strange going on at the front of the school?"

"No, not really...." Then he saw it. "Well, I guess we *are* in the Deep South.... It's a little weird." He went back to playing his PSP. Bryan's dad is Peruvian, so he thinks he's a little savvier about these things than I am. We saw the escort pull out in front of us, so we followed on our way to the concert venue.

At the venue a committee was there to greet us. They seemed nice, though now that my creepy-Deep-South goggles were on I was seeing everything through race and noticed that they were all white. They took us to a lovely brand-new backstage room to explain the evening's itinerary. In fact, the whole building looked brand-new. I said so as we were shown around and was told that they had just completely renovated this historic building to be the town concert hall, and that we were to be the inaugural performance. Flattered, the five of us and Bryan eased into conversation with the committee. They were all *super* friendly, and soon we were all joking and laughing. The committee people started chatting about the dynamics of their town.

"Weeeell," the chairman started in a swinging southern accent, "All of us around here kind of divide the town into three groups. There are the L.P.s, the D.L.P.s, and then there's everybody else."

"So who are the L.P.s and the D.L.P.s and all that?" Greg asked.

"Okay now," the chairman explained, "the L.P.s are the Lake People. Generally around here if you have any kind of money, you live on the lake. And if you have, well, you know," he dropped his voice in a mock-hushed tone, "a *lot* of money," back to full voice, "then you're the [Darn] Lake People!" He turned to the rest of the committee, and they all started laughing. We smiled politely.

He continued, "Now that I think of it, we're putting you up tonight at some really nice condos by the lake, so you'll get to be D.L.P.s too!" I wasn't sure if I wanted to claim this title just yet....

"And everybody else," he added, once the laughing had died down a bit, "well, there's quite a divide in this town between the *haves* and the *have-nots*."

"Hmmm?" I added, nodding my head with raised eyebrows in response. "And are there any...tensions around here?" I asked innocently.

"Oh, there are all *kinds* of tensions in this town!" he exclaimed. "You've only got white folks and black folks here, and they don't see eye to eye. And then you have the Baptists and the Methodists. You see, most people here are either Baptist or Methodist, and they *really* don't see eye to eye. It *really* creates some problems around here, you know, with the community coming together and such. I guess there are a few Catholics, but, well, you think the Baptists and the Methodists don't like each other, but they agree on one thing, and that's really having a problem with Catholics. There's only a few Catholics around here, though, and they meet way out on, what is it...?" Turning to the committee, "way out on Thorton Road or something? Anyway, kind of on the far side of town."

He paused here, probably remembering that we were Mormons.

"You know, you all are probably the first Mormons anybody around here has ever met," a committee woman exclaimed. "It's probably really good for the kids around here to see a Mormon for the first time. You know? We had a Jewish fella come through here, a musician like you all, just last year before this hall was finished with the renovations, and he stopped by the school, and we had to introduce him by explaining all about the Jewish people, you know, to make the kids more *aware*. Don't know when's the next time that'll happen, so we figured we'd better take advantage of the situation while we had him here!" Committee laughter all around.

We were all trying hard not to look at one another, because if we did, our mind reading would have revealed way too much on our faces. Bryan and I were digging our nails into each other's hands under the table in the secret way we do when we are either: A) appalled by what is going on, or B) in complete disbelief at what is happening. This was one of those rare moments when it was A) and B), and the only way to keep things under control was to smash our hands discreetly while smiling and nodding at our hosts.

"You know," the committee woman continued, "we are just so excited you all could come and open our season for us. It really is the biggest ticket in town right now!"

"Just out of curiosity," Melody asked, "are the tickets priced so that there will be a good mix of people at the concert? You know, families and students too?" Our booking agents usually requested this from the venues.

"Well, most of the tickets have gone to sponsors, and the few left over have been sold to season-ticket holders. We have a wait-list a mile long! You're the biggest thing to hit this town since Sherman!" She seemed really pleased, and the whole committee thought the Sherman comment was the funniest thing to hit *them* since, well, you know.

As much of a compliment as the Sherman thing was meant to be, I was getting a little worn out by all the racial references. Sherman was a general during the Civil War, a war in which the South was fighting to keep the slaves, when it came down to it. Maybe it's time to move on? Everyone could pack away their flags and call it a day. In case they hadn't noticed, Confederate flags kind of offend people nowadays.

We also knew that "sponsors" and "season-ticket holders" meant wealthy people. That night there probably wouldn't be any students and very few families in the audience. Without the generosity of patrons there probably wouldn't be any arts in this country, but we liked that most of our concerts were filled with families and students *along with* the privileged. That's why we had our booking agents request that at least *some* less-expensive tickets were available for students and families.

The committee woman continued, "Oh, this might be a good time to ask you all a question. Now, I know you like to go out into the lobby after concerts and sign autographs for the kids, but we sold special VIP tickets that included a special signing with The 5 Browns. So, you see, it wouldn't look very good if you just went out in the lobby and signed autographs for just *anyone*. It would really help us if you could go straight to the VIP reception following the concert."

Slight pause. All of us looked at one another and started to answer at the same time. We knew the answer to this question without deliberating. We try to be the "everyman's" classical musicians. We let audiences know that you don't have to be elitist or educated to understand, enjoy, and love classical music. We do school outreach for free, play school concerts for free, and DEFINITELY sign autographs for free. We told her that signing only for the VIPs would compromise our principles. Anybody who goes to our Web site knows that we always sign after our concerts. Signing only for the VIPs would make us hypocrites (and maybe D.L.P.s, but I didn't mention this).

Committee-woman tried to push it a few more times, making things a little awkward. As we were finishing the backstage tour and on our way to the soundcheck, she seemed to think that we would change our minds later.

The hall was adorable—small, but gleaming and new. Our five pianos were already arranged on the stage in the tightly configured position that we prefer. We can see and hear one another better when we play this way. Every time I walk into a concert hall, and everything is ready and waiting for us, I feel blessed. So many people do a lot of work to prepare things before we arrive, and I try to never take that for granted.

We rehearsed a little, with the committee anxiously observing offstage. We started by playing through parts that we wished had gone better at the last performance, and we worked for a balance of sound between us. No two halls sound exactly the same, so each performance has a slightly different acoustic setting. A soundcheck is basically a "heads up" to our ears, and a little bit of a warm-up for our hands, arms, and bodies. After thirty or forty-five minutes we decided we were tired and didn't want to wear ourselves out before the real thing. Usually after a soundcheck we would grab a quick lunch and let ourselves take a nice nap. Since we need to be most alert from eight to ten in the evening, we kind of depend on a rest to jump-start our night. As we started to gather our things to leave, I was already imagining a dark, quiet hotel room with clean, cool sheets, and me drifting to sleep...

"Well now," Committee-woman charges in, "We have just enough time to get you to the condos at the lake, changed, and off to the patron's reception!" Okay, so no nap; and maybe no lunch? I patted my stomach and made a tired face to Gregory when no one could see. He raised his eyebrows and nodded to show he was hungry too. We were all hoping there'd be food at the reception.

The condos turned out to be really nice. Those Lake People weren't kidding. The reception was to be just below our rooms at the country club. We changed quickly and headed down to the reception, which was already in full swing. I was just thinking how nice a three-day weekend on a lake would be sometime as I grabbed Bryan's hand and entered the soiree. At a patron's reception the artist gets a chance to meet the people who made the concert possible. Even when we're tired, and maybe a little hungry, we feel grateful to those who fund the arts. They are usually people who love music, like we do. So even when their tax bracket is way different from ours, we have something in common: classical music.

The reception looked like many others I'd been to, so I tried not to be shy and worked my way around the room introducing myself. I started shaking hands and thanking the patrons for bringing us to Oldtown. Bryan was by my side as we came upon an older stocky man, probably in his late 60s. He seemed jovial in the southern, Oldtown way I'd noticed in the town's inhabitants. Or maybe it was the wine glass "shlopping" in his hand as he gesticulated.

"Well, well! We certainly are excited about tonight's concert!" he began. I was eyeing the dangerous wine glass. I really didn't want to be toting wine-soiled clothing in my luggage for the next couple of weeks.

"Oh, well, thanks so much for bringing us here!" I said. "We're really excited to play tonight. I'm Desirae, and this is my husband, Bryan. He's a concert violinist, and he's actually going to be playing with me on the con..."

"*Five Browns and a Black!*" he bellowed in a thick southern accent.

I stopped short, and Bryan and I both kind of froze, confused. We smiled while making curious eyes at each other. What did he mean by that? Bryan was wearing a black velvet blazer...he had luxurious dark brown hair, nearly black.... What was this guy talking about? Bryan and I decided to continue smiling and laughed lightly, figuring he couldn't possibly have meant what was starting to flit across our minds. No...

As we waited for his raucous laughter to subside, a woman, tall and slender with short gray hair piled high on her head, crossed the room from the opposite side and joined us. I felt a little relieved and hoped to have easier conversation with her. She knew Stocky Man, so I started again with introductions.

"And this is my husband, Bryan. He's a violinist and will be..."

"*Five Browns and a Black*!" Her high, shrill southern voice screeched with laughter, and she and Stocky Man thought this was the funniest thing to hit them since freaking Sherman. And then Bryan and I knew. We weren't laughing to keep up pretenses this time.

"Yeah, well," I started as they laughed. I gave Bryan a we-gotta-get-out-of-here look. We quickly made up some excuse and headed straight for the exit, grabbing some shrimp cocktail on our way out for sustenance.

Once in the hallway we started half-laughing, checking in with each other.

"What the heck was that all about?" I started.

"I don't knooow!"

We tried to speak in half-whispers but were getting excited. "Did they mean what I think they meant? I mean, you're not black, but I guess maybe you're not white, either? I don't know, I never really thought about it."

"Naaw, they can't possibly mean...but what could they mean?" he wondered.

"I have no idea."

"I know." He raised his eyebrows and started nodding. "They smell my fear."

And I realized he was saying this only half in jest.

Bryan and I decided to forgo the rest of the reception. I was never the kid who skipped class, nor read the *CliffsNotes* instead of the book. So this was out of character for me. It felt more like we were making a break from prison, or living that scene at the end of *The Graduate* where Dustin Hoffman and the girl he loves are running hand in hand from her wedding. So Bryan and I ran down the hall and escaped the bizarro reception.

Since there really hadn't been that much time scheduled for us to be at the reception anyway, we went to our room and started preparing for the concert. We're classical musicians, not pop stars, so we do our own hair and makeup. (And to our credit, we've been complimented more than once by makeup artists and hair stylists for our efforts.) We've had different professionals do the job for us along the way and have learned what we like and don't like. Give us thirty, thirty-five minutes, and we're dressed and stage-ready.

At the appointed time we all met in the hotel lobby to go to the concert hall. Once we meet in a lobby, our schedule proceeds like clockwork. If you're even five minutes late you'll get a lecture from the others on the way to the hall. Most of us will do anything to avoid this four-headed vocal barrage that will ensue. Fear of being the lone recipient is usually enough to keep a person on time. Usually.

The boys have their way of getting their things to the hall and the girls have theirs. We all drive in the same vehicle, but there's a difference. The girls, we hang our concert clothes neatly in garment bags. All of our makeup, shoes, and so forth are placed in a bag and slung over our shoulders. The boys prefer a different method. If you happen to stay at the same hotel as we do, then you may see my brothers waiting in the lobby before a concert. You will wonder, Why are they carrying all that stuff? You will think, There must be an easier way. Take Gregory. He will wear a skinny 60s-style suit, looking nice, except that he is carrying, with one finger, a plastic hanger with a black vest on it, a pair of deep-red corduroy pants with a few other fingers, and a set of keys dangling off the last finger. In his other hand you will see a pair of black Converse sneakers (designated a finger each), with a black belt and hotel key stuffed inside one sneak, and the other three fingers holding a can of Giga Hold Freeze Hair

Spray (he orders the stuff online and has it shipped to him in boxes). And this is the organized brother. Ryan, usually one of the last stragglers down to the lobby, will barely be holding onto nearly all his possessions (including his PSP, which keeps him company backstage). And he will frequently drop said possessions en route. The top buttons of his untucked shirt are unbuttoned, with his tie draped over his shoulder in a last-ditch effort at keeping everything on his person. We keep telling my brothers that there is an easier way, and we nearly converted them after they took a subway ride through Tokyo in this fashion after a car service failed us. But no, there will be no surrender to the girls' side. They continue their ways in a show of solidarity.

We arrived at the concert hall with nothing out of the ordinary. The committee, having more important things to worry about on opening night, had left us alone. They rushed around, every once in a while popping their heads into our dressing rooms to see if we needed anything. They really were considerate.

The concert went off without a hitch. It was sold out, and the committee seemed very happy. After the concert, Committee-woman again tried getting us to go straight to the VIP reception. Instead we went straight to the lobby, giving the people there our free attention before giving the VIPs what they had paid for.

After the reception I thought we were finally done with strange little Oldtown, until I was reminded that they were bussing children in from nearby schools to hear us play a shortened concert the next morning. Honestly, with our experiences in this town so far, I thought we were going to give the advantaged kids one more advantage that the other kids in the town wouldn't get. Oh, well. Kids are kids, I guess, and they should have a chance to hear some good music.

The next morning as we pulled up to the hall, we saw busses unloading hundreds of students of color. We also saw a few white kids lining up to enter the building. Granted, they were wearing uniforms, but nevertheless it was looking to be a good mix of kids. Some of them recognized us as we entered the stage door and started calling out to us and waving. That was a good sign. That meant their teachers had already coached them on who we were and what we do. We would have a bigger impact on them this way. *This* was what we liked to do. We want to play for kids who, without us, may never hear live classical music in their lifetime. It was going to be an honor to play for them.

Backstage, we could hear the high-pitched roar of 500 elementary students chatting. The five of us peeked around the curtain to see what our audience looked like. It couldn't have been more different than the night before. My heart warmed and expanded. Maybe I had misjudged the old committee after all. As much as they held onto their old ideologies, maybe they had a hope for the future. Maybe they looked beyond themselves just enough to realize that we need to share the good stuff.

We started the concert to the roaring applause and cheers of the students. Playing for kids is definitely different than playing for adults. Kids are used to rock concerts or MTV, so they made us feel like rock stars as we played some of our most well-known music for them. When I wasn't playing I noticed a lot of students playing air-piano while banging their heads around. Not a bad impersonation of the five of us, really...not too far off. Near the end of the mini-concert we took some questions from the kids. Their questions ranged from if we lived in mansions and were millionaires to what we think about while we're playing. The things they asked made us laugh and broke our hearts at the same time. I hoped that we might make an impression on them. Maybe, they might take an interest and begin lives enriched with art and music. Maybe...

When I was ten years old, my parents took Deondra, Gregory, and me to see the finals of the Van Cliburn Piano Competition in Fort Worth, Texas. It is arguably the most competitive and prestigious piano competition in the world.

I remember the performances clearly, and was in total awe. Out of the six finalists, there was one girl. To this day the profession is dominated by men. Looking back, it is impressive that in 1988 there was a woman there at all. She made a profound impression on me, as I thought she played more musically than her competitors. I felt a connection with her. To my young mind, we were sisters in music. I rose to my feet in my first standing ovation when she finished playing. If she could become a professional pianist, I could too. Looking at the schoolchildren we had just played for, I was reminded of her and hoped that new childhood memories were being created now, in this audience. Maybe we could make a difference in one kid's life, black or white, privileged or not. Even just one, I thought with a smile, as the kids got to their feet and gave what was probably their first standing ovation ever.

* * *

Desirae and I prepare to audition at several music conservatories together but wonder if we're up to the massive challenges that lie ahead. Are we good enough to hold our own against prodigies from around the world, or will we crack under the most intense pressure of our lives?

THE UNLIKELY VISITOR

BY DEONDRA BROWN

New York City
March 1997

My mom always wanted twins. Desi and I are the next best thing—close sisters, only fourteen months apart, and inseparable growing up. She had a year's head start on me—I remember waiting in the wings for *my* monumental third birthday, when I would be officially old enough to start *my own* piano lessons. Mom made sure I had my own music bag and everything. I was a hard worker, a stressed-out little one, and before too long, I was nipping at Desi's heels.

We shared everything you can think of—friends, clothes, shoes, cars—you name it, we had it in common. As good as twins, we always thought. So when it came time for Desi to go away to college, I felt like she was stepping into the next stage without me. We had always gone through everything together, and now she was leaving me to begin experiences I couldn't share with her. But what, I then wondered, was holding me back from going with her? I decided that I wasn't going to let a few high school courses keep me from going at the same time, so I worked extra hard and planned on graduating just in time for fall classes to start.

But I got a little ahead of myself. First we both had to audition and get accepted to the *same* school. That would take some sort of miracle to pull off.

We narrowed it down to six music schools, and we each sent in six different college essays. Each application included a forty-five-minute tape of our piano playing, a requirement to see if we met the school's standards before being allowed a live audition. The tape round alone eliminates many students. Most realize they can't even play that much music. If our playing wasn't good enough, our dreams of going to any of these schools would be dashed. Or worse, what if they only invited one of us to audition in person? As everyone does, we had our top choice—our "musical" Harvard—the one school we had always grown up thinking was the best of the best. Juilliard. Even the name sounded intimidating. With only five percent of pianist applicants accepted, was it even worth the trouble? With such prestigious alumni as Kevin Spacey, Christopher Reeve, and Robin Williams in acting and Itzhak Perlman, Yo-Yo Ma, and Wynton Marsalis in music—was there any hope? Not much, but we figured it was worth a shot. Why not?

With my dad along for moral support we started our two-week road trip to six schools in four towns coast-to-coast, ending in the most important audition of all, Juilliard. We somehow had survived the fifty-percent cut of the initial tape round and were two of the remaining 175 students vying for the seventeen open slots in the piano program. I tried to push the thought out of my mind that this was the most important ten minutes in all of my seventeen years. My stomach felt like it was on the most excruciating roller coaster of my life, and I was starting to give credence to those mentors who had told me I was never good enough to get into Juilliard.

The place was as intimidating as its name. I always prided myself on being different, but as I looked at my fellow auditioners, I saw the same pale, blank faces staring back at me, and I wondered if indeed I was all that different. We each appeared to have the weight of the world on our shoulders as the magnitude of the situation was kicking in.

This was self-inflicted torture of the worst kind. Even our support systems seemed to be caving under the pressure. Parents paced back and forth, looking as if they were on the cutting block themselves. I looked over at my dad, who offered a comforting smile, and I felt grateful that I would still have a life after this, no matter what happened.

As if it couldn't get any worse, Desi and I were asked to leave our dad on the main level (where the parents were politely *told* to stay, so as not to intervene in the process) as they escorted us up to the third floor. The third floor scared me from the second I stepped out of the elevator. Stale and deathly quiet, it seemed to ask over and over the question that had been swimming through my head all day: What are *you* doing here? I sat alone looking down the hallways, wondering what other tortures they led to, and waited for the huge black door in front of me to open and my name to be called. And then it came. Finally, it came.

"Deondra Brown?"

I got up and took one step, trying to convince myself that I deserved to be here, like everyone else. Each step brought me closer to the voice that had uttered my name and to that huge black door, which seemed so much bigger now as I stood before it, my fate on the other side. I took a breath, realizing I hadn't done so since leaving my chair, and strode through that door toward a person with a vaguely familiar face who was leading me to another set of black doors. Great. I realized his face was not just familiar, but the music of his piano playing was even more recognizable in my mind. Oh, no. I had grown up listening to the legendary recordings of this man, and now I was supposed to play in front of him? I was planning a quick exit strategy even as I crossed a second doorway and heard the heavy black doors clunk behind me.

I timidly glanced around a huge all-wood room, a rehearsal room for the school's orchestra, and was ushered to a solitary piano at a healthy distance from one long table.

Seated at the table was a group of the most stern faces I had ever seen—each one as famous as the next, looking like they really couldn't care less if I was there or not. And this was just the first hour of their day.

I was asked to begin with any piece I wanted from my ninety-minute program, and so before I could execute my retreat, I dove in. After a minute or so, I began to relax ever so slightly and finished the first piece with very little trouble. They asked me to begin another, and then another. I got no more than a few lines into my third piece when I became keenly aware of a noise coming from the table. Was that scribbling I heard? Oh, no, what were they writing? And I could hear conversation now. Oh, no, what were they saying?? As I tried to focus on what I was supposed to be thinking, the scrap of confidence I had left was beginning to fade. I wasn't sure how much longer I could keep it all together, but before I knew it my ten minutes were up. I'd somehow survived.

There was nothing to cling to—no feedback at all from the jurors, not even a faint smile of encouragement to get me through the next several dreaded hours. All I could do was wait with the others who auditioned, until a sheet was posted with the names of those performers they wanted to hear again. As if going through this once wasn't enough. If Desi's and my name weren't there, our lifelong dream of going to Juilliard would be abruptly over, and we'd be forced to imagine our lives without it. One silly sheet of paper was going to determine our whole future.

We sat and waited for what seemed like an eternity. Some frantically paced up and down the hallways while others sat and stared at the wall. One girl, prompted by her father, even laid out on the floor and attempted to do some strange relaxation exercises, hoping that each breath would bring her that much closer to the peace we all sought. But peace was not to be found anywhere that day.

And then there it was. People crowded tightly around the list. Before Desi and I could get close to it we noticed eyes splattered with tears, the type that only come from dashed dreams. Our anxiety spiked as we pushed our way through the crowd toward the tiny piece of paper. But there they were—*Deondra Brown*, and right below it in alphabetical order, *Desirae Brown*. The relief was overwhelming for a brief second, before the familiar anxiety sank in again, this time with distinct dread and painful fear. This was different from the first audition—they wanted us to prove that it was no fluke the first time. I had so much more to lose, so much more to prove now, as I was that much closer to being accepted. Ouch.

The practice rooms just made it that much worse. I was surrounded by amazing pianists, all cramming in last bits of practice—geniuses sharing thin walls with me, yet never missing a note, and not remotely as fazed by the pressure as I was. Second-guessing my abilities at this point was a given. The waiting was proving to be my biggest enemy.

As I tried to compose myself in a vacant restroom, I finally caved to the pressures of the day and crumpled to the floor of my stall in quiet hysteria. *Tap, tap.* I gathered myself up off the floor, wiping away my tears, a sure sign of defeat, and timidly opened the stall door. Looking down at me were two of the kindest and most gentle brown eyes I had ever seen, on a face that radiated love and concern. I was a little taken aback, considering the privacy of my situation. But I was quickly filled with awe by those loving eyes.

There in front of me stood a woman whose face was worn with the experiences of time far spent. She was dressed in a faded green cotton dress that seemed to hold as many stories as her weathered expression. She said with a heavy Jamaican accent, "God loves you, child, and is watching over you. Don't even worry another thought, because I promise, you'll be back here next fall to start a new chapter in your life."

With another genuine smile, she was gone out of the bathroom just as quickly as she had appeared, and I was left to gather my thoughts. My mind reeled with the words she had meekly offered, and the timing of it all was enough to keep my mind turning for years to come. Just as I was succumbing to my crippling self-doubt—the point of no return as far as a performer is concerned—I had received these personal words of comfort. I closed my tear-filled eyes and silently offered up the most humble words of thanks I could muster. I asked for the strength I would need to persevere through the rest of the day. As I quickly wiped my eyes again and went to face the music, the words "You will be back next fall" continued to ring in my ears.

I walked into that audition room with a confidence that was all but forgotten to me—the confidence that comes only from realizing that, as alone as I may feel, I am never on my own. I guess I need to be reminded of that once in a while. There is a strong power at work beyond our control; a *subtle* reminder is sometimes necessary.

✳   ✳   ✳

Toys crammed in my pockets and hidden all over the house just seemed so...necessary.

THE PLAYER PIANO

BY RYAN BROWN

Alpine, Utah
Summer 1994

"Mom, I'm done."

"You're done? How long did you practice?"

"Two hours."

"Really? I didn't hear you practicing all that time. What were you doing in there?"

"I was practicing...really!"

"Hmm. Did you do your sight-reading, your *Hanon*, your competition repertoire, and your old music?"

"Yup!"

"Really? I don't think I heard you going over all those things. Sounds like things were kinda silent in your practice room throughout the day."

"Nuh-uh, I did do it all, Mom," I said in a slightly whiny voice.

"All right then, let's see what progress you made today. Your teacher wants you to have these things worked on, and all she cares about is your improvement."

Panic washed over my face. Oh, no. If only I would have practiced the entire two hours and learned all the things I was supposed to. It's going to be a long day. Now, since I didn't practice these things very well on my own, Mom was going to practice with me, and she always wants everything perfect for my lesson.

As we all know, kids exaggerate when it comes to doing their work. Any kind of work our parents give us just seems like their way of picking on us and trying to make us unhappy. I always had trouble practicing long hours like my older siblings. Three hours a day just seemed like way too much.

As I got older, I realized that my parents just wanted me to be good at something and work for something that could benefit my upbringing. It's not that I didn't like to play the piano; it's just that I would always get distracted and mess around. As my mom would say, I had the attention span of a gnat! I always hated it when she said that. I didn't quite understand what that meant. All I knew was that it was not good.

My typical work schedule for the day was to practice, and then Mom would ask how things went. If I didn't practice long enough, or she couldn't hear me practicing in my room, she would check up on how my music was going. I know this sounds totally harmless. But it really wasn't. I was a pretty bad kid. I would skip pieces and exercises just because I didn't want to do them, and at the end of my practice I would hope and pray that Mom wouldn't listen to my music because I knew it was going to be dreadful, and that meant she'd sit with me until I got it right.

Day after day it went on like this, with me sloughing off my practice, then Mom checking up on me afterward. If I had worked on my pieces diligently, my full practice-time would have gone from four hours to two. I just kept falling into the same trap, day after day after day.

You may ask what I was doing in that room when I was supposed to be practicing.

Well, I tried to be as secretive as possible, because it actually made practice kind of fun. Every day, early in the morning, the five of us would call pianos for that day. The people who called the pianos first got the best ones. I didn't care about the best piano. I just wanted the piano in my room so I could be close to the hundreds of toys I had begged my parents for, hoping for a chance to play with them when Mom was gone or not listening. I got away with it for a while, until Mom noticed the lack of sound coming from my room. Being on the top floor, I tried to cover this up. As she walked toward my room to check up on me, I could hear the "thump, thump, thump" of her footsteps at about twenty paces. I had enough time to hide my toys, jump on my bench, and pretend I was in the middle of one of my pieces.

One day, Mom opened the door and said over my practicing, which I had started five seconds earlier, "Ryan, what are you doing in here? I haven't heard anything coming from your room for fifteen minutes."

"I've been practicing. I swear! See!" I played.

"Hmm. Well, you better practice hard so I don't have to check up on your music later."

"Okay, Mom, I will."

As you know, a mother can read her kid like a book. I figured out that when she said, "You better practice hard so I don't have to check up on your music later." I knew then I was doomed, and that she would be listening to my work at the end of my practice time. I needed a plan so that I could play with the toys in my room without her knowing it.

First of all, the piano I always used in my room was a special one—it could play back something you had just recorded. It took me a while to realize the possibilities of this. Of course, a kid my age, with my predicament, is going to do the obvious—record himself practicing and play the music back as long as he can get away with it. I thought I was a genius. I'd make the piano work for me, while I did what I loved most—playing with Legos and army-men. I pulled this off for quite some time, thinking I could never get caught, it was such an elegant dodge.

One day, I heard Mom walking toward my room. I barely heard the footsteps this time over the piano and the explosions my mouth was making as I played with my army-men. I jumped on my bench and started trying to play the recorded music. The five seconds I had before she reached my door were tough. Trying to catch up with the notes was not easy because the keys were all moving already. It was the least I could do to try to cover up my scheme. I thought I was done for the first time Mom walked in, but somehow I faked well enough with the player piano that she just walked in and walked back out, thinking I was practicing like a good little boy. I knew that it was only a matter of time before I was caught, but I was going to push this piano as far as it could go.

Weeks passed, and still I held my secret. I couldn't believe it was lasting this long. During these weeks she never checked up on any of my pieces because she thought I was practicing long hours. Life was beautiful; things couldn't have been better. Playing with toys during practice and Mom not listening to any of my music was just so awesome. About two weeks later, I found out that she knew more than I thought she did.

"Ryan, it's been a while since I've heard your music. You've been practicing such long hours, things must be going well!" she said.

"Sure, Mom, yeah, things have been going good," I said, trying not to sound scared.

"Well, maybe we should hear a few things today."

"But why? I've been practicing so much!"

"Well, we'll just hear a few things."

"Fine...."

I was caught. Later that day as she listened, I was quite horrendous. She called me on it.

"You were recording your music all this time, weren't you?"

I didn't fight it. She was smart.

"Yeah, Mom," I said. "How did you know?"

"Because I kept hearing the same mistakes over and over and over again, nonstop."

"Aw, man, you really can hear everything a mile away, can't you? It's not fair."

"Oh, yes it is. You're grounded for a long time, buddy."

I was never allowed to practice in that room again; nevertheless, sneaking army men into whichever practice room I used just seemed so natural.

Gosh, I was a lazy kid sometimes. All I wanted to do was have fun. I'm grateful for what my parents did for me back then. Playing the piano wasn't always easy, and it's nice to know that I always had someone there who cared about my talents when I didn't.

✳ ✳ ✳

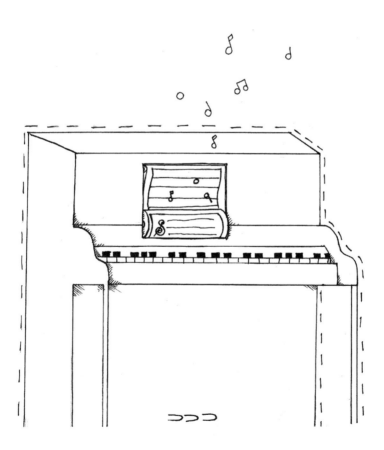

We Browns are like any normal kids, except we happened to start taking piano lessons at the age of three. We had our good days and bad days like anyone else. We worked and played hard. Because of our efforts early on, from as far back as we can remember, a pattern began to form for the rest of our lives. But that didn't mean it was always easy...

OPERATION FIND RYAN

BY DEONDRA BROWN

Houston, Texas
Summer 1989

We all have so many things in common—the same fair skin, light eyes, and even the same smile, we're told. We've all got amazing training from Juilliard and scored the same record contract and performing career. We share an understanding about how it feels to have a bad lesson, and how it feels to be disappointed in yourself for a mediocre performance. These are things that most people can relate to, but we really *get it* because we've all *lived it* in such a similar way. For brothers and sisters, we've realized over the years, this is a bit bizarre.

As parallel as our lives have been, though, we are as different in personality as two strangers waiting for the same subway in New York City. We have different work ethics, different practicing strategies, different goals, and definitely different ways of dealing with the stress of it all. Some of us have a more natural ability with the piano while others are more hardworking and determined to get things right. But we tend to mesh well as a group in the end. It just works somehow.

I don't know a kid out there who truly enjoys practicing. There's always a parent or two behind the scenes enforcing a schedule to help their child set goals and accomplish them. If you ask us who this motivator in our lives was, you will get the same resounding answer—Mom. But if you ask her, some of us made her job a little easier, and others made it a little more *eventful*.

We moved quite a bit growing up. It was almost never far, but just far enough to have to pack the entire house up in boxes. We never collected too much stuff, because we would have to move that much more with us the next time. And we never let the boxes stay packed for too long after moving, either. We tried to slide back into normal life as soon as possible. We had the routine down to a T.

It was another ordinary move—nothing too memorable. Just a few blocks away into a house with a better financial value than the previous one. It was kind of a thing for my parents to sell the home we were living in for a nice profit and move into another that they could make a killing on a few years down the road. They looked at it as a good investment opportunity.

We were really excited about this new place because it was bigger than the previous one, and as a sweet bonus, it had an awesome swimming pool in the backyard. In the humidity of Houston, a swimming pool was a must during the summer. Apart from practicing and quick breaks to eat, we would spend every waking hour playing made-up games in the pool or pretending to be mermaids. This was before my brothers realized that it's not really cool for boys to be mermaids, but even still, they played along and were good sports just the same.

During the summertime, before we could head out to the pool for a game of "Marco Polo" we had to get our practicing done for the day. We got up in the morning and raced to fulfill our obligations so we could go outside. No use dragging it out and wasting all day. We never really argued because we knew practicing was just something we did, like waking up for school. It's not negotiable. Ryan, being the youngest and only having started piano within the past year, hadn't quite figured this out yet.

One morning we all woke up as usual and went into a normal rotation to give everyone sufficient practice time on our two pianos and one full-size keyboard. We had begun with only one piano in the early years, but we eventually outnumbered it as more of us turned three and began taking lessons. At one point there just wasn't enough time in the day for all of us to practice. Now that we were lucky enough to have more pianos, there were no more arguments, and everyone had sufficient time. Eventually it was Ryan's turn to practice, and being only four years old, he required Mom's full attention. One day Ryan was nowhere to be found, and after a thorough search of the house, she brought in reinforcements to scour the premises and secure the target.

We split up and searched every room, closet, and under every bed. We walked around the backyard and then the neighborhood calling his name. He was still pretty little, but definitely old enough to know better than to pull a stunt like this. We called and called, getting more and more frustrated that he was wasting *our* precious swimming time. Boy, was he going to be in trouble. *Big trouble.*

And we said so, too, as we began to look inside cupboards and cabinets, yelling threats as we searched. This was really not funny anymore. What a punk, I thought. If Mom doesn't kill him, I think I will. I never would have thought about making such a fuss over an ordinary day's practice. I knew my responsibilities and always made sure they were done. I was definitely one of *those* in our family.

On our third lap around the house, I secretly began to get a tad scared. What if something bad had happened, and here we were yelling at the poor kid? I pushed that out of my mind as I began looking in even more ridiculous places this time around. Some cabinets are even too small for a four-year-old, but that didn't stop me.

And then it came to me. I ran downstairs into the storage room and began looking inside the few remaining boxes there. I made my way through each box with no success. In the back corner of the room I opened the very last box. Smiling up at me was one very naughty little boy. He had found a nearly empty box and shut the top flaps to hide himself from his responsibilities that day.

"I found him!" I yelled to the others, proud of myself. He was really going to get it this time. I was certain of it. Mom put her arm around him and said, "You ready now to go and practice?"

I was baffled and deflated. It's not that we like to see one another get punished, but with the trouble he had put us through, it seemed impossible that he would escape it. It might have made me feel a little less angry at him if there had been some consequence to this hideout, some justification for our ordeal. Operation Find Ryan was now over, and it was as if it had never happened.

Later my mother explained to me that she had felt just horrible that day. The fact that Ryan was hiding from his practice worried her, and she didn't want to be *that* mother—the dictator with no concern for a child's real wants. She spoke with Ryan after we had all scattered and discovered that it wasn't practicing the piano that made him smuggle himself into a box. He simply wanted to play with his toys, and that's what he was doing when I found him. This was just a day when a talented little boy was being just that, a *little boy*, a normal four-year-old kid.

* * *

"No...please don't do it. It's not worth it. You could get hurt."

"Nah, you'll see, it'll be awesome. Don't worry so much."

QUEEN OF THE HILL

BY GREGORY BROWN

Cemetery Hill
Alpine, Utah
Winter 1995

As a kid who spent the first half of his childhood in Houston, Texas, I can tell you that snow was a magical and elusive thing. During these first eight years of my life, there were only a handful of days when the weather cooperated enough to bring us unlucky tykes from the south the wonderful gift of a snowy day. I vividly remember those winter days as more exhilarating than Christmas morning because they came far less often and lasted half as long. What snow we did get was never much, though. In order to make a snowball of any decent proportion, you would have to slide your hand across a few feet of ground before you could collect enough to throw. Good aim was therefore of utmost importance in a Texas snowball fight, as ammo was always pitifully scarce.

And don't even get me started about snowmen and sledding. Sledding in flat East Texas is much like the summer activity of Slip 'n Slide. A running start and a belly flop could not only buy you a few feet of skid but a nice grass stain on your winter coat as well. Snowmen were out of the question too. While other states get visits from every kid's favorite frozen friend, Frosty the Snowman, I don't believe he's ever been brave enough to set foot in the south. The closest thing we ever got in Texas was Frosty's much less jolly distant relative—Slushy the Severely Deformed Snowdwarf.

One day when I was nearly eight, my dad came into my bedroom, sat on my bed, and asked me what I thought about moving to Utah. At first the thought of leaving home was a scary one, but all I needed to hear were the words "mountains" and "snow," and I was sold.

By the time I was twelve, winter in Utah had become, without a doubt, my favorite time of year. We moved into a house right across the street from Cemetery Hill, the absolute best sledding action in all of Alpine, and kids would come from all over town just to sled on "our hill." While having this hill right across the street was a kid's dream, it could also be extremely tormenting.

You see, in my family you couldn't go out and play until you had finished all of your schoolwork and piano practice. There were plenty of hours early in the day to do this work before the other kids got home from school, but inevitably there would be days where one or more of us would slack off. During winter, these were the really hard days. Since most of the five pianos in the house were close to windows (to shed more light on the keys), if you didn't finish your work when the other neighborhood kids finished theirs, you would be forced to watch them living it up every time you glanced out the window. There it was, the most fun any kid could ever have, waiting for me right outside my door, and here I was, sitting on a hard bench, trying to speed-practice through the last of my agonizing *Hanon* exercises and double scales because I had fallen asleep on the keys for an hour earlier in the day.

Falling asleep on the keys has been a favorite pastime of mine for as long as I can remember. It's a great way to draw your work out for the entire day. Mom was wise to me, though, and she would come into my room every now and again to see why she hadn't heard music coming from it in a while. As the door would open, I'd snap out of my dreaming and sit up straight, acting like I had been studying my music score the whole time.

"What have you been up to?" she'd ask.

"What do you mean? I've been practicing."

You'd think I would have realized that my glazed eyes and the bright red piano-key impressions on my forehead gave me away, but somehow I always thought I was pulling one over on her. Those naps were so satisfying (I still indulge in them today), but once mid-afternoon rolled around, and the kids began to sled, I'd curse my *Hanon*-induced narcolepsy.

Melody was always "the good kid" growing up. She did her work when she was supposed to, she was always prepared for her lessons, and she most definitely would never have been caught drooling on the keys. Beating the other kids to Cemetery Hill was therefore never a problem for her. She would either be the first one there, honing her skills alone while her slacker brothers pouted in their practice rooms, or she would patiently wait for us to finish so she wouldn't have to go by herself. When I finally finished my work, I would run down to the garage, throw on my snow clothes—still damp from the previous day—grab my sled, and run up the hill as fast as possible to join Melody.

I was convinced that I had the coolest sled on the hill. It looked like a shrunken black snowmobile with a bright red "1" on the front of it. I was known by the Cemetery Hill regulars as pretty fearless because my sturdy and well-balanced sled was perfectly suited for landing jumps that few others could. I kind of let this get to my head, and it eventually caught up to me.

For a year I had been preparing for a piano competition that a lot of kids around the country (and their teachers) take really seriously. You first compete in the state competition, and if you win, you go to the regional competition. If you're fortunate enough to win there, you head to the nationals and compete against the winners of the five other regions.

This particular year, I was lucky enough to have made it all the way to the nationals. One day, about two months before the competition, I was up on the hill sledding with Ryan, Melody, and a friend, Cassie, who took lessons from the same piano teacher. Cassie was the apple of every thirteen-year-old boy's eye, and she just so happened to be my closest friend. I was pretty proud that she didn't mind being seen with me, but even though I *had* mustered the confidence to hold her hand once, we were only ever "just friends." The other guys on the hill didn't know this. All they saw was some cute girl in stylish snow clothes being all chummy with the piano kid from across the street. Guys left and right tried to show off all day to get her attention, and it was obvious that she was quickly becoming Queen of Cemetery Hill.

Seeing an opportunity to impress Cassie and simultaneously impress the other boys by making them think she was my girlfriend, I became suddenly infused with more confidence than I had ever had in my young life. Black sled in hand, I took my swagger to the top of the hill and prepared myself for "Dead Man's Jump."

Dead Man's Jump was the most vacant slope on the hill. It was a terrifying run that most kids were too scared to attempt. The terrain on this particular part of Cemetery Hill was shaped like the ski-jump slope that you see during the Olympics: a nearly vertical drop, then a slight incline, and then a sharp drop-off. On the right day, a kid could easily get six feet of air at twenty miles per hour.

Well, it must have been the right day. As I sat down on my sled, Melody called up to me, telling me to wait. She reached the top of the hill, breathless, and crouched next to my sled, putting her hand on my arm.

"Gregory, I don't think you should do it. The hill is way too icy today, and you won't be able to control your sled. Plus, the landing is gonna be really hard."

"Oh, come on, I've done this tons of times. I'll be just fine."

"No, seriously, please don't do it.... It's not worth it. You could get hurt."

"Nah, you'll see, it'll be awesome. Don't worry so much."

At that, I took a deep breath and kicked off.

Halfway down the hill, I realized that she was right. I was picking up way more speed than I ever had before, and I was starting to veer out of control. Terrified and at the mercy of gravity, I hit the jump wrong and the sled began to tilt sideways in the air. There was no escaping it—this was gonna hurt real bad. I hit the ground, landing awkwardly on my right arm, and the breath got knocked clean out of me.

I lay there motionless, trying to fill my lungs, and heard feet scurrying in the snow all around me. "Are you all right? Are you hurt?" I looked around to see who had witnessed this humiliating wipeout. Sure enough, Cassie was standing there, joined shortly thereafter by Ryan and Melody. Trying to act like the tough guy I wasn't, I told them I was fine and just needed to walk it off, but my arm was in so much pain that I knew I wasn't fine.

Instead of walking it off, I beat a path home, eventually slipping past my siblings and Cassie unnoticed. Once I was out of sight, I lost it, and the tears began uncontrollably. Not only did my arm hurt really bad, but I knew I had just put all of my hard work in jeopardy, with nationals just around the corner, and my teacher would kill me if I had to back out.

"Yep, it's broken" were the doctor's words. My parents looked devastated by the news. According to the doctor, the chances my wrist would heal in time for nationals were slim. He suggested I take some time off in order to heal right. Not only did this mean no practicing, which was actually an exciting thought, but it also meant no sledding.

For the time being, the latter was the much more bitter pill to swallow.

It wasn't enough to deter me from the hill, however. Despite my cast and the discomfort, I still suited up with Melody and Ryan every day and headed up the hill. I couldn't sled, but I'd rather watch them than sit at home by the window.

Melody's Cemetery Hill weapon of choice was much less flashy than my black sled. It was this flat, tiny, one-by-one-and-a-half-foot turquoise pancake with a little white rudder in the front that let her steer. Seeing as though the dang thing was so small, the only way you could ride it was to stand on it, squat, and hold on to the front rudder. Everyone who ever attempted setting foot on it never made it more than a few feet down the run—that is, everyone except Melody.

Melody is sort of the known klutz of the family. There are plenty of stories throughout our years of growing up that end hysterically with cries of "TIMBER" ringing through the air or her lying face down in the middle of the Times Square subway station, but this is not one of those stories. Melody and this little runt of a sled seemed to have some sort of miraculous chemistry that challenged everything we had come to know about her physical coordination—or should I say lack thereof. She could not only tame the mini turquoise beast, but with it, she could fly down the hill faster than any kid in all of Alpine, Utah, while making turns on a dime at the same time. It really did defy all logic.

As I was now incapable of going down the hill myself due to my broken wrist, I just sat there in the snow, bewildered by her ridiculous skills. When I was healthy, I was usually far too preoccupied with trying to pull off my own dumb stunts to notice what a talent she had. It was also the first time that I saw what was going on around me on the hill. Every group of boys that passed by me was talking about the "turquoise girl."

As a kid, turquoise was Melody's favorite color, so naturally her winter coat was also made in that best-of-all-colors (as was her favorite stuffed bear, whom she called Turk). That coat was probably *the* ugliest thing ever created by people who make coats. It was baggy and ratty, and she wore it so often that it was also dingy and discolored. My brother and sisters and I absolutely hated that thing. It made her look like a transient hobo girl from the slums of 19th century London or something. All she needed were fingerless gloves and soot on her face to complete the picture.

Despite her tomboy appearance and social-suicide attire, every boy on Cemetery Hill was in awe of the "turquoise girl." How had I never noticed this before? Every time she reached the top of a run and prepared to push off, everyone would stop what they were doing and watch anxiously as she zoomed by. I began eavesdropping on conversations around the hill:

"Did you see the turquoise girl make that turn at the bottom of the run? I've never seen anyone take it at that speed before!"

"That's gotta be the smallest sled I've ever seen in my life. How is she staying on that thing?"

"Who is that girl, anyway?"

During the time of my sidelining injury, I could see things clearly for the first time. Growing up, Melody was my overly mature, tomboy little sister who tried to talk me out of doing stupid things while still managing to have fun doing boy stuff. I always looked up to her and appreciated her for this—her unusual combination of sweetness and roughness around the edges—but somehow, I just assumed that none of the other boys would care to notice her. She assumed the same thing: that she just wasn't flashy or flirty enough to stand out. As it turned out we were both way wrong.

Winter rolled on that year, and my cast came off at last, about a week before nationals. My arm was still weak, but I came home as the alternate to the winner, so I wasn't too disappointed. Best of all, however, I could bring my black sled up to the hill and take part in the fun again.

While Dead Man's Jump was the furthest thing from my mind during the last days of that winter, and Cassie was at her home a half hour away, I realized that those things didn't matter so much anymore. I had been so bent on trying to impress the other kids on the hill by getting the highest air on jumps or by dating the cutest girl, that I never allowed myself to see that these things were, more or less, a waste of time. I can't remember the precise day it happened, but I finally understood that I had been the second coolest kid on the hill all along and had just failed to realize it. As the snow began to melt, I knew that I was the brother of the "turquoise girl," and that knowledge was all I really needed.

The other kids on Cemetery Hill came and went, the Cassies of my life held my hand and were gone, piano competitions were won and lost, and Alpine winters turned to spring, but through it all, that little girl with the dingy coat was always there to warn me when the run was too icy or to help me get up when the landing was hard and painful. Somehow, she always knew the right thing to do, even when I was too blind to see it. She didn't need Dead Man's Jump, she didn't need a flashy black sled, she didn't need a coat that fit, and she didn't even notice the boys noticing her. All she cared about was making the turn at the bottom of the run and having fun with her two brothers.

As I walked home from the hill with my sled on the last evening of snow that winter—dusky sky a dim orange and the smell of transition in the air—I stood in front of my house, thinking about how much I loved everyone inside. Through the window, I could see Dad making a fire in the fireplace and the girls on the couch sipping hot chocolate and wassail, watching an old movie. Ryan was on the floor playing with Legos, Mom was making dinner in the kitchen. I stood there in the snow, watching them for a few minutes, wondering if they really understood how much I cared about them, how much I needed each one of them. Finally, I took a deep, contented breath, picked up my sled again, and pulled it into the garage. There, hanging up on the wall hook, was Melody's old turquoise coat, soaked from a full day of sledding and looking just as ratty as ever. It was the very thing I had made fun of so many times, but it didn't look quite so ugly anymore. Instead, what I saw there in our cluttered garage that night was my little sister, my sledding buddy, and my best friend. I hung up my coat next to hers, and as I opened the laundry room door, I thought:

"I wonder if she even realizes that she rules Cemetery Hill?"

* * *

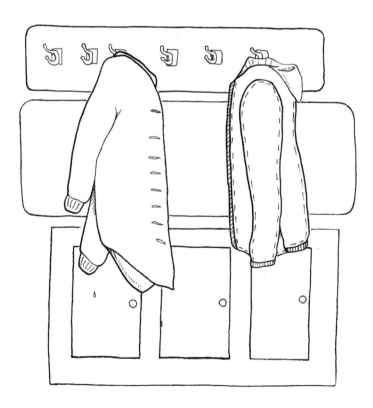

Deondra and I were always close growing up. Pictures show us hand in hand smiling as toddlers, playing duets as kids, and arms around each other in Times Square as teenagers when we auditioned for Juilliard in New York City. I know what the future holds. Two grandmas smiling back at the camera, just the same way.

TWIN-ER DRESSES

BY DESIRAE BROWN

Houston, Texas
1980s

I remember the rain coming, and that Mom was gone. All we knew was that it was going to rain, and our swimsuits were going to get wet. I don't remember why, at seven and eight years old, Deondra and I were so concerned about the suits getting wet. In our childhood minds there must have been a very good reason. We had left them out on the diving board to dry after swimming earlier in the day, when the sun had still been out. It seemed like a brilliant idea at the time, and we thought ourselves quite clever. The suits had been left to dry while we went in the house to finish our practicing. Then we noticed the clouds—dark and quickly rolling over the backyard. We ran to all the doors that led into the pool area, but of course they were locked when our parents weren't supervising. Our brains raced. There must be a way in to grab the swimsuits before it rained. We realized that the only way in would be over the locked, gated fence around the outside entrance to the pool.

I remember running with Deondra out of the house and around to the back of the yard. We stopped short, right in front of the towering gate.

"How are we going to get over it?" I asked, breathing hard. The wind was blowing, carrying the storm. We had to make a decision fast.

"We're going to have to go over it," Deondra said definitively.

"You mean climb it?"

"Yeah." She was so sure and confident that I was a little taken aback. Usually Deondra, the younger sister, liked to play it safe. I typically made the tough decisions and looked out for her. Time was running out, though, and we had to move. At that moment we both looked down at what we were wearing. It was unfortunate that we were both wearing our favorite outfits. The outfits that Deondra and I loved the best were little dresses that were exactly alike. We called them our "twin-er outfits." We wanted to be twins, and felt like true twins when we went to school or played with friends in these dresses. That day we were wearing our very favorite "twin-er" clothes—identical little lightweight denim culotte dresses with a white flower pattern. We realized there was no time to change.

Then Deondra did the bravest thing I had ever witnessed her do.

"I'll climb over first. I'm taller than you. I'll go over and grab the swimsuits. You can help me back down the fence when I come back."

I was aghast. She wasn't just risking her safety; she was risking her *dress*. If she was taller than me, it was only by the slightest bit, and I knew it wasn't a deciding factor. Part of me knew I should be the one sacrificing, taking the risk, but I let her do it.

She was a really athletic kid. In school we would have to run the mile every few weeks. Our un-athletic-looking P.E. teachers would teeter uncomfortably on undersized children's chairs and time us with stopwatches. All of us schoolkids admired those who ran the quickest mile. I dreaded running days and would run near the back of the pack, dragging my legs and loosely flailing my limp arms. Deondra, though—she saw running the mile as a challenge that she was going to take down. She wasn't an outgoing kid, but everyone spoke with reverence about the girl who ran the fastest in her grade. Only one kid ran faster than Deondra, and he was a boy.

As I faltered by the fence deciding whether to let her climb, she was already scaling the iron bars. As she got near the top of the fence, it looked as though she was going to make it. It really did. But just as she was rounding the top, the back of her dress caught the iron bar, and we heard a heart-stopping rip. I gasped, and she froze at the top of the fence. This was so much worse than wet swimsuits. This meant Mom finding out, and explaining, and…the ruined outfit. My stomach sank. I still had my perfect dress, but my sister didn't have hers. I felt terrible.

Deondra slowly climbed down from the fence, abandoning her attempt. When she was safely off the fence we inspected the dress. It was bad, unsalvageable, and we knew it. I expected her to start crying, but she courageously said it was her own fault and that she would tell Mom. I said that it was my fault and that I was to blame. Being the oldest kid in our family, I never knew what it felt like to have a protective sibling until that moment.

We walked without words back to the house as the first drops of rain began to slap the pavement of the driveway. My sister might as well have taken a bullet for me that day. Her bravery and generosity astounded me. In her way, she had sacrificed her favorite thing in the world—for me.

* * *

Two photographs sum up my childhood experiences in music. Both were taken at the biggest piano competition I ever entered growing up. Although the snapshots depict the outcome of the competition, the true story lies behind the flowers, medals, and smiles.

BUGS

BY MELODY BROWN

**The Stravinsky Awards
Champaign, Illinois
June 1993**

A life in music was and will always be incomplete without competitions. Or so I was told. They were necessary in helping us progress in our music since they created goals and deadlines. The Stravinsky Awards was the Olympics for young pianists. It left an impression on me that would last all my life.

My dad happened to take two pictures that would come to define the pressure of the competition. The first was the list of finalists, where almost every name would go on to be a classmate of ours at Juilliard. The second was Gregory sitting with the winners of his division at the awards ceremony. To his right were two who would later become the most talented pianists of our school. And to his left, smiling, was one of the great pianists of our generation, Yundi Li. No wonder crazy quirks started to emerge in me. The level of competition was so high.

When I got nervous as a kid something strange would happen. The feeling we've all had of bugs crawling on our skin plagued me even when there were no bugs to show for it. I was constantly brushing and slapping at my face as a result. You can imagine what it looked like when these nervous spells would come on.

With the countless complexes recognized in psychology, I ventured to guess that I could've been diagnosed with something tangible at my young age. Knowing what caused the problem might've alleviated years of slapping at my face. My only theory is that when I was two or three years old living in Houston, Texas, our church had a big water party for all of the kids, and I remember looking down at my bare foot. Hundreds of fire ants were climbing up my leg. My mind froze; would they bite my hands if I wiped them off? I ran over to my dad, who was talking to a Sunday school teacher. He didn't see or hear me. I waited until he finally noticed me pulling on him. "What's wrong, Melody?"

The ants were covering my leg. Shocked, he ran me to one of the baby pools. Immediately the ants released their miniscule jaws from my leg.

That night, although my mom lathered on medicine, the stinging pain from the tiny red bites was unforgettable.

Are the ants to blame for those "bugs"? If only I had found a cure before they started to infiltrate my piano playing. The result was touching my face relentlessly while in mid-piano playing sentences. It plagued me when I was really nervous. These were times of recitals, major concerts with orchestras, or big international competitions. Risking downfall by my hands going from the keys to my face to the keys and back again was difficult choreography that neither judge nor audience could appreciate.

My mom eventually realized it came down to my hair. After all, this was what I was brushing at. When a tiny, wispy strand of hair would stroke my cheek, it sent warning signs to the brain that something was on my face. My mind pictured ants. I *had* to get them off. Mom took quite a bit of time fixing my hair before big events. She made sure every lock was out of my face, giving me a sort of hair-sprayed helmet topped off with a bow. When I entered one of the most important competitions, she crossed her fingers and hoped the helmet would hold.

The Stravinsky Awards was an international piano competition for kids. I was about nine years old when I first entered. We made a family trip out of it, since each of my siblings was competing as well. For us it was a big deal to travel all the way to Illinois to compete against kids who had come from places like China, Germany, and Russia.

We showed up the day before the official competition week, in awe of what was before us. Some kids and families had already been there for a week! Parents were clamoring over the best practice rooms for their kids, urging them to sneak into the competition rooms to try the pianos, and ultimately finding any way to get the maximum amount of practice time for their little prodigies.

My parents dropped us off at the practice facility, helped us get our rooms, and left. In my nine-year-old mind I was old enough to practice on my own, but walking down those hallways made me realize that I was the exception. I tiptoed up to each room to see if it was empty and saw parent after parent yelling at their kids in Russian, English, Italian, Chinese, and Korean to name a few. My parents knew how nervous and excited we were. They also knew that this atmosphere of competition was enough to push us into practicing well. This was supposed to be *our* achievement.

Once the competition started, the atmosphere in the hallways was incredibly tense. Chairs were lined up. The judges were a few feet inside listening to hours of competition. Every kid dealt with the stress differently. There were those who paced up and down the hallways before they got called in to perform. Seeing them go back and forth got annoying if you chose to sit while waiting. There were also those who meditated. Their loud breathing and closed eyes set them apart. No one wanted to sit next to a meditator. Finally, there were some who shamelessly put their ears to the door, trying to hear if they were better than the person performing inside.

I was one of the kids sitting and waiting, though I wouldn't have looked too normal either. I was the girl with incredibly slicked hair, wearing a pretty floral dress with ski gloves on. Our hands were always freezing before we performed, no matter what the temperature of the room. We owned multiple pairs of ski gloves and wore them at every competition.

I was already starting to feel the "bugs" coming on. When my mom saw a ski-gloved hand going for the meticulously plastered hair she had just fixed, the emergency tools were broken out. This bag of tools consisted of rubber pads (sadly, there were times when the bench slipped out from under us), snacks in case we got hungry, water in case we got thirsty, lotion in the event our hands were dry, towels in case they were sweaty, tissues, Band-Aids, fingernail clippers, liquid bandage, and lastly, her trusty comb and bottle of hairspray. She took the latter items out and sprayed away at my helmet. The braid no longer felt like hair, but a crunchy rope. The top of my head was supposed to be indestructible.

When I could touch my hair and it felt crispy, I knew the spraying had to be almost done. Thank goodness Gregory's voice broke the sound of aerosol echoing through the tense hallway. "Be careful, the piano is sort of stiff and muffly, and one of the judges looks like a scarier version of Maleficent." I was about to compete in the same room, round, and division where Gregory had already performed. He wanted to protect me from any of the surprises he had found. In good spirits from his earlier performance, he tried to pump me up before going in. "Oh, also the pedal's a little stiff, and…," he paused in the middle of his inside scoop, "there are *tons* of parents and teachers in there." Great. I hadn't known the competition room was open. Didn't they know it was hard enough to perform in front of just the judges?

I performed three works of music before I got to my last piece, Mendelssohn's *Songs without Words*. I was nearing the end when I realized I was almost done. That's never a good thought to have, since it pulls you away from your focus. I started thinking about the judges and the fact that I was kind of hungry. I began to see the faces of parents in my mind, praying for me to make a mistake. Then, it happened. On this occasion it was the actual popping of a glued hair. It was on the left side of my face. The vision of ants flooded my mind. The pressure to get them off was uncontrollable. Fitting in a slap to my face posed a problem. Anyone familiar with Mendelssohn's *Songs without Words* can attest to the left hand's difficult fluid passages accompanying the easier "song" or melody that takes over the right hand. I should've used my right hand when it was free, but it seemed like more work to get it over to the left side of my face. Hence my left hand would have to accomplish playing beautifully and killing the "ants" all in one.

As you can imagine, it was impossible. The ants won. They took out my left hand, leaving it stranded. I floundered for what seemed like a while but miraculously found my place before the end. When I finished the performance, I ran out. The judges later commented on how I even forgot to bow.

I was frantic to find my mom. She would never hear us play growing up. She chose to wander the halls to find a nice, quiet place to pray her heart out.

"Mom?" I found her sitting on the stairs. She stood up, looking a little dazed.

I knew that look so well. I'd continue to see it years down the road. Her concerned eyes would either turn more concerned with my next few words, or they would relax with relief. Sadly, this time her eyes were actually tearing up, because of mine.

She held me in her arms, trying to comfort me, when Gregory and my dad finally caught up. They looked at me, surprised I was crying. My dad was sort of laughing. "You have no idea! You did really well!"

"But what about the mistake? It was right at the end!"

"It really wasn't as bad as you think," Gregory chimed in.

Finally my mom's eyes looked relieved, and she smiled, hugging me tighter.

The first round was over. I didn't think I stood a chance of making it to the finals with a mistake. A part of me was sad that I wouldn't get to wear the pretty new dress my grandmother had bought me in case I made it. Seeing it hanging up in the dorm room that night made me relive the mistake over and over in my head.

On the morning of the fourth day, the list of finalists was posted. I still remember how nervous I was walking up to it as others were already walking away with victory fists in the air. I expected to be one of the kids who left with drooped heads, burying a teary face in the arms of a teacher or parent.

I scanned the list for my age division. Right below "Gregory Brown," I saw it. My name was actually there. I was stunned. How did I make the finals of my first big competition when I messed up? There must have been a mistake. I was in a daze when Gregory came up behind me, jumping. He gave me a big hug. "We made it!"

To this day, the final round is a blur. I can see myself in the big performance hall wearing the blue velvet dress my grandmother gave me, but I recall little else on account of the stress.

We barely made it in time for the announcement of the winners. A kid named Dusty, by far one of the most talented students in our Utah piano studio, needed our help. He was always hilarious, but this time he wasn't joking. He couldn't find his black dress-shoes. And more than likely he would be receiving one of the top prizes on that stage. When digging through the soda cans, candy wrappers, and pizza boxes in his dorm room turned up nothing, he employed our help. We dispatched a team of kids to find "Dusty's black dress-shoes." We scoured the lobby, dozens of kids' rooms, the practice rooms, the bathrooms, the cafeteria—everywhere!

It was hopeless. He started thinking someone was trying to sabotage him. Finally we had to leave him before we missed the announcements. We felt bad as we left him standing in his black suit and white socks.

Out of about thirty kids in the finals, I had a low chance at placing. Since there were six esteemed places and two honorary awards, I had eight chances of getting *something*. Of course I hoped my name would be called last, the impossible dream of getting the gold medal. I was just settling into this dream when I heard it: "And the honorary award goes to Melody Brown."

I didn't place, but I still had high hopes for Gregory. In my mind he deserved to place at least in the top three. I began sending good vibes in the judge's direction, to no avail. Sixth place was announced, and he walked up to accept his reward. To my surprise, he was ecstatic. Later he told me he felt extremely lucky to have received any award.

Other names were being called while I sat staring at my prize, a manila envelope. I pulled out a certificate when my eye caught something else—the words "One Hundred Dollars." I had just received my first check for playing the piano. This was a strange realization. Playing the piano was just something I did and loved. Could I ever make a living out of this?

Hearing the name "Dusty" and "second place" brought me out of my stupor. We started laughing uncontrollably when we saw his feet. He walked onstage for the prestigious award wearing blindingly white sneakers. Some kids barely cracked a smile, while we all laughed and cheered.

The winner's reception was incredibly boring. One by one, the competitors started disappearing. You'd see Dusty whispering in their ears, and then they'd vanish. Before we knew it, we couldn't hide from the adults anymore. They laughed when they finally found us downstairs, playing tag. The last kid standing upstairs was the little girl who won my division. Being a gold medalist, it was somehow beneath her to run and play. I still remember the smug look on her face when her parents led her to the stairs, saying, "Go play!" It was starting to look bad, as if she was a poor winner. We weren't going to *force* her to play.

We continued our games, when gradually she started running and playing too. The memory of us all chasing one another, the sweat dripping down Dusty's face, the neckties on the carpet, the dress-shoes discarded all over the place— this was the end of the Stravinsky Awards. There was no more pressure, no more walls between competitors. We were all just kids: running, playing games, being ourselves.

* * *

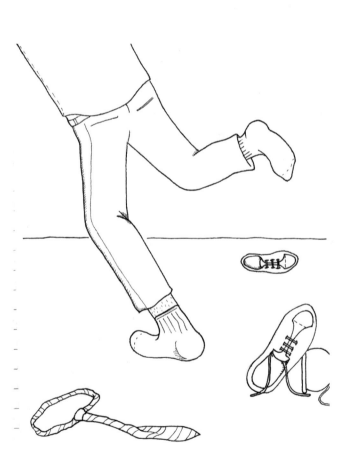

Sometimes personalities clash within a family. It doesn't mean you don't care about each other—it just seems to be a fact of life in a close-knit group. We all know the right buttons to push, and sometimes we risk losing more than we ever imagined.

THE LEARNING CURVE

BY DEONDRA BROWN

Alpine, Utah
Fall 1993

Gregory and I have always been each other's antithesis. As kids I was the type who worked rigorously to be prepared for my piano lessons. I practiced until I got my assignments done, even if I knew my teacher wasn't going to ask me for all of them at my lesson. I was determined to get everything just right. I never thought twice about it. Gregory was very different, at least until his early teens. He had a knack for knowing the bare minimum he could get away with: enough just to fly under the radar. It really was quite a talent.

And he was so outgoing and friendly growing up that he learned to talk his way out of just about everything with our piano teachers. He'd just crack some funny joke and divert the situation until its magnitude was lessened. It was amazing how our teachers could continue to fall for it over and over again. I, on the other hand, didn't have that ability. I was quiet, shy, and a little awkward. I tended to crack under the pressure of my own expectations. I could beat myself up forever over any little thing; Gregory just let things roll off his back and went about his life as if nothing at all had happened.

That is, until the day when Mom assigned me to start checking up on his daily practicing. To her it made perfect sense—the responsible one looking after the irresponsible one. Desirae and I were old enough so that Mom wasn't practicing with us anymore, and Gregory and Melody were fast approaching that age themselves. Mom thought it would be a good idea for Desi and me to hear some of their assignments at the end of every day to make sure they were on the right track and preparing for their lessons. It would save her some precious time in the day and provide us with valuable experience teaching others. After all, before too long we would be old enough ourselves to start teaching. Why not give us a bit of a head start? Why not go to the dentist to get a cavity filled while I'm at it too? It felt close to the same.

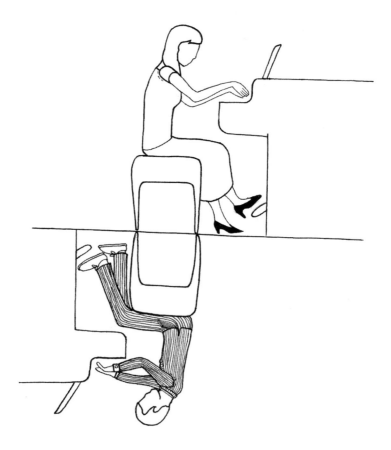

"So, let's hear some scales," I began. I figured we'd start off easy before delving into the meaty assignments. I might as well be fair and give Gregory a chance to work up to the difficult stuff. After several scales came and went with mistake after mistake, I realized this was going to be a long night and *far* worse than I'd expected. And I'd anticipated it to be pretty bad.

I made him suffer through each scale over and over until it was perfect in every way. Mom had asked me to do a job, and I was going to do it right. I was a soldier all the way. Insults began to fly from each side as Greg and I wondered how we could *possibly* be related. The only thing we seemed to share was a propensity for being stubborn. I insisted that it needed to be done perfectly, and he was equally insistent that it was good enough. We went back and forth for hours. How on earth was this ever going to work?

After a battle of wills, I grudgingly relented, deciding I'd heard enough of what were *supposed* to be his scales. I wasn't going to sit there all day pointing out the obvious. This was unproductive for us both. I asked to hear the main piece he was learning, a long and difficult one by Mendelssohn, knowing his lack of preparation was going to reach a whole new level. And did it ever.

With the music in front of him, Gregory began. Or at least, he tried to. It sounded as if he were reading it for the first time, probably because he *was* reading it for the first time. It hardly resembled anything Mendelssohn would have written, much less imagined. My anger and frustration brewed more with each wrong note and rhythm. The "music" petered out; he could continue no more. He had to know what was coming. Mom had given him a couple days' notice to get everything in order, but in regular Gregory fashion, he decided he'd deal with the consequences later. And later was now upon us both.

And so I lost it, yelling mean things left and right, hoping to injure him. And he yelled back insults about how mean and bossy I was. This was our daily routine. We both had legitimate frustrations, to an extent, but you couldn't have explained that to us. We were too passionate and headstrong to comprehend that one of us wasn't right and the other wrong. And regardless, we were too young to care.

But we could be fighting one minute in a practice room, and the next minute be laughing and riding bikes and jumping on the trampoline—it was that radical of a switch. Fifteen minutes after he'd play his last note, we were friends again, knowing nevertheless that the situation would repeat itself tomorrow. But we always put that in the back of our minds. We'd deal with that tomorrow.

But after a while, even the most fun afternoon's play outside couldn't erase the bitterness in our practice sessions. One day it came to a head. It started out like any other session together. We fell into our normal quarreling, but today was far worse, painful to the core. Amid a volley of horrible words, we stopped mid-insult, and fell silent into deep thought. We had come to a critical point in our relationship, and we knew that how we handled things this moment would determine many things in the future. Even as young as we were, we realized we'd stooped so low that it frightened us to visualize what we were capable of, where we'd end up. Was it worth the cost to be the one who's right? If we were to be on speaking terms years down the road, we knew back then, we would have to start changing *now*. There was no time to waste. We both felt the urgency. We were still young and figuring things out—we had to give each other that—but that was no excuse.

I said a few words that seemed to encompass the problem.

"Is all this *really* worth it?"

Gregory's answer surprised me. After all, he was only eleven.

"No, because we love each other."

And we did. We both knew it beyond a doubt. We vowed then and there not to let our differences ruin what we had as brother and sister—that we would never let anything drive us apart, as had begun to happen. We shared the blame. We would need to find a way to appreciate each other for those things we *did* have in common, and put our personalities aside. If we could find a way of being patient with each other, despite our faults, we knew everything would be okay. We knew that our relationship would survive.

And practicing together just had to go. Even Mom realized it after hearing the daily yelling and witnessing the consequences to our friendship. It would be too tempting to fall back into old habits. Besides, we were doing each other and ourselves far more harm then good. Gregory and I needed to be brother and sister for a while, not teacher and pupil. We needed to make the effort to start fresh, and we did.

Sometimes in life you have to learn things the hard way, and Gregory and I did just that. I wish I could say from that day on I was a new person, but my patience will always find some way of being tested. I will always set expectations too high. Gregory and I had an early opportunity to reflect on the importance of priorities. All five of us deal with similar instances daily when we rehearse our five-piano music. As hairy as things sometimes get with five *very* different adults working together, we always remember the importance of keeping our relationships strong. We are brothers and sisters before anything else.

We made a pact early on, even before we were The 5 Browns, that we would never let our careers or success come between us as siblings. Everything we know would be challenged some way or other, we were sure of it. We must never take for granted those closest to us. People will do their best to pull us apart, planting seeds of jealousy and doubt, and try to proclaim one of us as a bigger star than the others. But it is up to us how we handle these situations, whether we let someone undermine our goals and determine our future. We've seen what this industry can do to family members. We are just too important to one another to let that happen. We would sooner give it all up entirely.

Although we have changed dramatically since we were children, Gregory and I have come to realize that we will never be able to fully understand each other and the way we react to certain situations. But as long as we can appreciate our relationship and the great things we each bring to the table, and let the rest fall by the wayside, we can always be the type of friends we would hope to be as brother and sister. Opposites or not, we have learned how much we mean to each other. Isn't that what ultimately matters anyway?

* * *

Even though I knew the game would be gone, I opened it up anyway, just in case a cell phone miracle had somehow occurred. Sure enough, there was nothing there but the time, the date, and my piano- key wallpaper. Game over—998,653.

FALLING BRICKS

BY GREGORY BROWN

Denison University
Granville, Ohio
Winter 2004–Fall 2006

Our first concert at Denison University in Granville, Ohio, had been an absolute nightmare. It took place when Melody, Ryan, and I were still in school in New York, while Desi and Deondra, having just finished their master's degrees, had moved back to Utah with their spouses. The five of us had been booked in Granville, one of the cutest college towns in the country, before we had really made a name for ourselves. Those days, the existence of The 5 Browns was known only by my family and our record label, RCA Red Seal. We had just signed our five-CD recording contract and were in the process of working out the logistics of arranging pieces for five pianos, as such arrangements were more or less nonexistent.

During the week leading up to the concert, I was beginning to feel both nervous and excited at the thought of playing at Denison. I had been working on a new piece with my teacher at school, and it was just getting to the point where the music was sounding good to me. When a piece begins to sound good to yourself, you know you're on the right track, because every pianist is definitely his or her own worst critic. I practiced as hard as I could in the days before the concert, seeing as though you never know exactly what issues might make themselves known once you're under pressure. None of us had a ton of performance experience at the time, so getting up on a real stage in front of real people who paid real money to hear you play was an unsettling thought. All the same, I was feeling pretty good about my chances of being able to put my best foot forward on the stage at Denison University.

Melody, Ryan, and I decided to book our plane tickets so we would arrive in Ohio on the morning of the concert. We had classes all the previous day, and the school made it very hard on you when you missed classes, even for a performance. The morning of the concert came, and the three of us woke up to one of those rare New York snowstorms that only occur once or twice each winter. We knew this was going to make our day a ton more stressful, so we hurried our packing, hopped into a cab, and headed to JFK airport. On arriving there, luggage in hand, we checked the flight board, only to have our fears confirmed. Almost every flight was delayed or canceled, and ours was delayed at least an hour. After waiting at the gate for over two hours, we were finally allowed to board the plane and take our seats.

Six hours later, we were still sitting in those seats, but the plane had yet to leave the runway. Planes were taking off only during random calm intervals, and there was a traffic jam of them waiting to go. Just as our plane would inch closer to the front of that line, the de-icing agent they douse the planes with in such weather would wear off, and we would have to leave our place in line and de-ice all over again. We went through this about six times—one for each hour we sat there—until the airline gave up and canceled the flight altogether.

During the ordeal, we kept in touch with my older sisters, my parents, and the presenters of the concert, all of whom were in Granville freaking out at the prospect that we might not make it in time. We would get their hopes up every hour or two by relaying the captain's news that "we should be getting the final clearance for wheels up in about twenty minutes," but after five of these announcements failed to amount to anything more than another de-icing, everyone in Granville was forced to begin brainstorming a contingency plan for the dreadful scenario that was becoming more likely with each passing hour. "If the other three Browns can't make it, what do we do?" There was only one answer—Desi and Deondra would simply have to take over the entire concert on their own.

Normally, this wouldn't have been all that big a deal. Desi and Deon had been playing two-piano music together since they were little kids, and this wouldn't be the first time that they shouldered an entire program on their own. In fact, before the five of us became The 5 Browns, my two older sisters played quite a few concerts as a duo. After we signed our record deal, however, we collectively decided to put solo and duo career plans on hold to concentrate on the group opportunities at hand. This meant that, in many ways, we would have to adjust our practicing priorities to accommodate these new, unexpected career goals, and therefore the upkeep of a lot of our preexisting repertoire would have to be put on hold. Though our concerts and recordings as a group still include what could be called our first love—solo and duo performances—our focus now is on equality and sharing the spotlight as an ensemble. So a concert of duo music was the last thing on my older sisters' minds when they flew into Ohio that day, and the reality of it took them completely by surprise.

In a panic, they called their husbands back in Utah and had them fax over music that they hadn't looked at in quite some time, hoping that it would still be in their fingers. They frantically rehearsed in the hall during the remaining hour before the concert, and then performed in front of a sold-out show.

In performing circles, this is the perfect nightmare scenario—the kind of crisis you know might happen to you one day though you hope and pray it only happens to someone else. That said, my sisters pulled it off despite their near-breakdowns, and the concert went just fine. In fact, it came off well enough for the presenters to ask us back two years later.

Turns out, a lot can happen in two years. Where the five of us had been a bit lacking in performance experience at the time of our first trip to Granville, we had a good couple of hundred concerts under our belts by the second time around, and the situation was much less stressful. There were no snowstorms, no delayed flights or frantic faxes, and no, I wasn't going to get off the hook this time while my sisters took one for the team.

Even though Granville is not all that big of a place, we were still really looking forward to going there. We saw it as a chance to show the people there who we really are and redeem ourselves with a concert that, most likely, we would be much more prepared for. As the plane left the tarmac on the morning of the concert I felt a strange relief. We were actually going to make it there this time.

With a chuckle to myself, I opened my cell phone in hopes of passing the flight time by playing a few games. I had recently downloaded one of my all-time favorites, Tetris, onto my phone, and this was the first time I had really gotten the chance to sit down and play it. For those who aren't familiar with the absolute bliss that is Tetris, let me take this opportunity to help you understand its beauty.

Tetris is a puzzle-game that has been around since the '80s. The object is to run up your score as high as you can before the game gets the better of you. There is no end to this game, as far as I know, and it lasts as long as your skills do. Different configurations of bricks fall from the top of your screen, and your job is to stack them as compactly as you can as they reach the bottom. Stack the bricks all the way across the screen without any gaps, and those bricks will disappear, but leave gaps here and there, and they'll build up closer and closer to the top. The longer you go, the faster it gets, but once the stacked bricks reach the top, it's game over.

To my surprise, I made it through the entire two-hour flight without the game besting me. I also managed to survive the drive from the airport to Granville as well as the breaks in our soundcheck without those bricks reaching the top of my screen. I was racking up points like crazy and blowing away my previous record by tens of thousands.

While on tour, my siblings and I have a routine. After our afternoon soundcheck, we'll go back to the hotel for some downtime and a nap before the concert in the evening. Well, as we got back to our hotel that day, I sat on my bed, unpaused my game, and continued playing. I figured I'd just take a shorter nap than usual after my game finally ended. The problem with that logic, however? You guessed it; my mad brick-stacking skills were way too ridiculous for my own good. I ended up playing straight from the end of the soundcheck all the way to dinner. I even took my phone with me to the table and played through dinner, hardly eating as much as I should have.

At last, it came time for the concert. I continued stacking bricks backstage—foregoing my warm-up routine of soaking my hands in warm water, stretching my arms out, flexing my fists, and massaging my palms and knuckles. This routine has saved me in many a situation where the concert hall doesn't have a piano to warm up on backstage (as was the case at Denison University), but who needs to warm up when you're getting closer and closer to breaking the ever-elusive 1,000,000-point threshold?

The concert started out okay, but I could definitely feel that my mind was a little fuzzy. I figured this probably wouldn't be a huge problem, as we had played these pieces quite a few times already that season, and the chances of a meltdown were slim—or so one would think. After I finished each piece, I'd rush backstage to my phone and continue where I left off, playing Tetris through all the solos and duos that didn't include me, and throughout intermission. By this time, my brain was mush. You can be confident that you've reached a new level of pathetic when you close your eyes and all you see are funny-shaped bricks falling from the attic of your imagination. By the end of intermission, I was at 998,653 when I had to go back onstage for the second half.

The opening piece was "Scenes from *West Side Story*," one of our most popular five-piano arrangements, one which we had played probably a hundred times before our second trip to Denison. So many venues requested it after our first season that we decided to add it to our second season program as well. I could probably have played the piece in my sleep, and on this night I would have been better off if I *had* actually played it in my sleep. At least then my mind wouldn't have been raining bricks in front of my eyes.

The piece begins with the five of us snapping our fingers (I know, corny, but come on, what's *West Side Story* without snapping?). I sat down at my piano bench and got ready for Desi's cue. Things started out pretty well—our snaps were perfectly in sync, and we followed with the quick back-and-forth between four of the pianos. A couple of bars later, the back-and-forth returns, and when it was my turn to enter the fray, all I could see were Tetris bricks, and consequently I froze up completely.

Freezing up at this part is like removing one domino from a row of dominos and expecting them to keep falling. It began a five-piano pileup with each person playing on top of another, colliding in awful dissonances, while others snapped randomly without any decipherable rhythm. I wish I could have seen the looks on all of our faces as we attempted to rectify the musical carnage. Eventually, we all sort of petered out until the only thing left was an awkward silence (and maybe the chirp of a solitary cricket in the distance). We looked at one another, and then Desi mouthed the word "beginning" and gave another starting cue. After the restart, the piece continued without a hitch, but the damage was done. In all the hundreds of performances of five-piano music that we gave over our first couple of years of touring, a piece had never completely fallen apart onstage like that.

I was mortified. I knew it was my fault, and worse yet, I knew it was all because of that dumb game. My mind had become a wasteland of falling bricks, and I could hardly even form a complete thought anymore. During the rest of the second half, I didn't have the guts to pick up my phone again. My siblings well knew the reason my brain was out to lunch, and if they saw me playing it again, I would just draw more attention to it. I left the flip phone open on the dressing room table and figured I'd wait until I got back to my hotel room to see what happens when you reach a million points.

The concert finally ended, and as usual, we came back to the dressing room for a minute or two in order to grab a few things, and then we headed to the lobby to meet people and sign stuff. I glanced at the phone on the table as I walked out of the dressing room door and had one last pitiful urge to pick it up and play, but I knew it would have to wait until after the signing.

A little over half an hour later, I rushed back to collect my phone, eager to find out at last what the game would do considering there wasn't room on the scoreboard for a seventh digit. I couldn't wait to master the game with no ending. What would it do? Would the score roll back to zero? Would it simply stop? Would it declare me Tetris champion of the world? After a full day of stacking bricks, I was at last going to see what lay behind the velvet curtain. I hurried into the dressing room, and as I stepped in, something caught my eye. Flowers? "Wait a second…there weren't flowers in here before. Someone's been in here!" My heart jumped into my throat, and I turned to look at the table where my phone was. Where just half an hour ago it had been open and on, it was now closed. All I could do was stand there in disbelief as I stared at the ugly, out-of-date little cell phone, which hadn't been closed all day. Not only had I messed up a concert because of that thing, but now I didn't even have something to show for it. I walked over to the table slowly and picked it up. Even though I knew the game would be gone, I opened it up anyway, just in case a cell phone miracle had somehow occurred. Sure enough, there was nothing there but the time, the date, and my piano key wallpaper. *Game over—998,653.*

For such a small city, Granville holds a big place in my mind when it comes to unfortunate touring situations. While the first concert ended in an admirable effort by my sisters, the second ended in me pathetically sabotaging my siblings and instigating the biggest mistake we've ever had onstage. Since that day, I've never played another game of Tetris. I just haven't had the desire to waste another day of my life, especially if it means going brain-dead onstage and making a fool of myself. I just wish that I could have found the person who closed my phone, so that I could've tied their shoelaces together or something. The image of that closed phone is something I have yet to fully recover from. I guess I deserved it, though.

Maybe, if we're lucky enough, we'll have another chance to go back to Granville and do things right. If we do get an offer for that "third-time's-a-charm" concert opportunity, let this go down as my official promise to the people of Granville, Ohio:

1. I will not book a flight that arrives on the morning of the concert.

2. I will take my pre-concert nap.

3. I will eat my dinner.

4. I will do my warm-up stretches.

5. I will not think about bricks, I will not stack bricks, and I will most definitely refrain from imagining myself stacking bricks while playing the piano.

Feel free to hold me to it. I'm pretty sure I've learned my lesson.

* * *

The five of us have no understudies—at least not yet. I have been to Broadway shows, excited and straining with desire to see my favorite legendary artist perform, only to flip open my program before the show and have a little paper insert fall to the floor. After trying unobtrusively to retrieve the fallen slip of paper from between the narrow rows of ancient theater seats, my heart falls when I read the announcement that Herbert Newel will be replacing the lead. Herbert Newel! Who's Herbert Newel?

DOES THE SHOW HAVE TO GO ON?

BY DESIRAE BROWN

Knoxville, Tennessee
April 2007

Oh, oh no. Here it comes. I jump out of my hotel bed in the dark and run to the bathroom. I really, really hate barfing. After being sick I slump, weakened and exhausted, on the floor.

"Hey, Babe, are you okay in there?" my husband Bryan asks in a muffled, sleepy voice.

"No, I'm not."

"Can I do anything for you?" he asks.

"I don't think so. I'll just have to play it out and see if it passes."

I crawled over to the bed, pulled my pillow off and dragged it on my hands and knees into the bathroom. Might as well get settled in.

This scenario played out many more times before the night was over. I had never been this violently sick before and couldn't guess how long it would last. I also had never been this sick before with a concert to play the next night.

What happens if a person is so sick she can hardly walk, yet 3,000 people have already bought tickets to her concert? Do you cancel? What happens when you cancel? Do people get their money back?

I remembered the night before. I'd had a delightful time. We had gone to dinner with the board members of the concert series. Bryan was with me so we had an especially fun time. Our dinner companions had been engaging and interesting people. We decided Tennesseans were especially friendly people. The restaurant was fabulous as well. I even ordered filet mignon and mashed potatoes with those skinny, curly fried onions on top. Delicious. All and all, a really great night.

But not anymore. Being this sick was demoralizing. I felt so human, so...disgusting.

I vaguely remember Bryan carrying me back into bed sometime during the night. I think he asked if I needed to go to the hospital, but I answered by falling asleep. The next morning was no better. The day began to pass in a delirium of sickness. I foggily remember my dad and Bryan talking over me while I tried to rest. I couldn't focus on what they were saying because of the screaming ravage in my stomach. Sometime later Bryan pulled some medicine and a Gatorade out of a paper bag. He must have found a pharmacy. After much cajoling, Dad and Bryan reasoned with me that it was imperative that I rehydrate. They explained that I had the choice of drinking the Gatorade or, if I refused, going to the hospital. I decided that the hospital seemed like a lot more trouble, and drank the darn drink.

Since I was awake to drink, we started going over our options for the concert.

"So, do you think you will be able to play the concert tonight?" my dad asked.

"Seeing as I can hardly walk the distance to the bathroom, I'm gonna say no." Why do I have to be such a smart aleck when I'm sick?

"Well," he continued, "before you completely make your decision, I think I should let you know that the proceeds from this concert are going to be given as scholarships to music students in the area. Apparently there have been some kids accepted as music majors to the university, but they can't afford it."

Just my luck—the one concert out of hundreds that I want to cancel has to be for a good cause. I groaned in bed.

"Oh, I don't know, Dad...." I had visions of me spewing vomit all over the stage.

He continued, "If there's just any way you could maybe play on even a few numbers it could work. The others could throw in a few extra pieces, and the show could go on."

I couldn't help but think of the grand visions of kids going to music school because of me...but there was no way. I reached up and touched my greasy, matted hair and my clammy face. Even that motion made me want to be sick over the side of the bed. But the kids....

I lay there and thought about it. I'd done things before that I thought were impossible. Getting into Juilliard for one. Keeping up at Juilliard for another. I also remembered walking into the largest recording studio I had ever seen in my life with a legendary record producer waiting for me. I was so paralyzed by nerves, intimidation, and expectation that I thought there was no way I was actually going to be able to record for Sony/BMG for the first time. It seemed so impossible at the time. I mean seriously, who would want to hear *me*? Why was this record company spending so much money and time to record *my* playing? Would I be able to play even one note under the pressure?

Sometimes I get in these moments where it seems like time is going to stand still, like there's no way the moment will get to play itself out—it's just too impossible. I stand there in the moment and think: Will I ever be on the other side of this impossibility? Will I ever be walking back to my hotel after recording with a legendary record label in the largest recording studio in New York City, and actually be happy that everything went well? To push the moment through, to actually play it out, I have to push myself in a way that feels like jumping off the high dive as a kid. You stand there on the dive-platform, the sun blinding your eyes, thinking there is no way your own body can fly through the air at such a height, propelled to such depths. You are alone. You can see your parents' mouths moving but you can't understand what they're saying. Only you can make this happen. And then something else takes over. You find strength that is not yours, and you are flying the way you do in your favorite dreams.

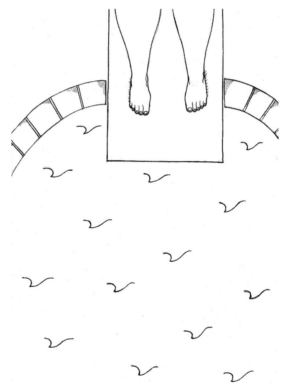

Bryan and Dad waited patiently for me to think everything over. This was probably difficult, considering I was staring blankly at the wall. Then, like a reflex, I just decided to do it. I would play the concert. I still thought there was no way I physically could, but I just decided to commit to the impossible. If it was possible at all, it would be one of the hardest things I had ever done. I just decided to have faith, I guess—on one condition.

"Okay, I'll try," I blurted out to Dad and Bryan before I could change my mind. "On one condition. We have a serious prayer right now."

I'm impressed, looking back, that I even managed to put a little makeup on. I dragged myself to the bathroom mirror, stopping every minute to sit and rest on the floor, and lean over the toilet again. Bryan even helped me curl my hair with a curling iron. Now that's devotion. I put on my gown but passed on the heels for a pair of flip-flops. Bryan handed me the room's trashcan on our way out. Nobody wanted an accident.

Our ride to the concert hall tested my resolve to the brink. I know the sweet board member assigned to drive us only had the best intentions, really. But I thought I was going to lose it when Bryan opened the door to her car, and the smell of "dog" literally whooshed out.

"Why, you don't look that bad at all!" she exclaimed. "The board is going to be so relieved!"

"I apologize for the car being a mess," she continued. "I take Muffin around with me everywhere. I just can't stand to leave her alone." Bryan whispered quickly to just get in and pretend that everything was normal. The smell was overwhelming, and the dog hair coating the seats had me reeling. I took a breath and climbed in the car. I didn't want to be sick in her car, but it was inevitable.

"Oh, oh no, honey. We'll get you there, fast," the driver said as she punched the gas. I don't think she was as confident in my appearance anymore.

When we arrived at the concert hall, the concert committee greeted us with smiles. I rudely walked past them to lie on the sofa in the green room. Every concert venue has a green room where the artists can chill out and relax. It very rarely has green carpet or walls, and I often wonder who came up with calling it a green room. Lying on the sofa, I hoped the concert committee would understand that my actions were for their own good. A repeat of the car experience would have been uncomfortable for everyone.

I turned on my left side and tried to lose consciousness. I'd heard somewhere that lying on your left side helps calm a stomach. It wasn't working, so I pretended I was asleep and inadvertently eavesdropped on a conversation out in the hall.

"Yeah, I heard one of them's pretty sick. Been throwing up."

"Yeah…. If she's here, though, it can't be that bad. Performers, you know…." Chuckling. I could tell from the detached tone of voice and accent that they were probably stagehands. I didn't blame them, really. If I spent almost every day of my life running around to meet the needs of performers, I probably wouldn't take them seriously either. I'd heard lots of diva stories on the road, and how would the stagehands know if I was being a diva or not?

"Bob seems to think she might just be pregnant. She's got a husband with her." Light belly laugh.

"You think? Hey, what do you want to bet she comes back next year with a kid?"

Then a voice from down the hall. "Hey, what do we got bets going on?" He was approaching while he talked.

"Oh, I was just tellin' Wilkins what you guessed about her being pregnant." Bob must have been joining them. "We were about to bet on it. You in?"

"Sure, I'd put ten bucks on that." Bob was in.

"Ten for me too," Wilkins said as their voices started to move down the hall.

Then another voice called from the opposite end of the hall. "Hi, are you James?" I could hear my dad ask. "I was told I could ask you about a lighting issue…," he was saying as their voices trailed down the hall and out of earshot.

So they thought I was pregnant. If I had energy I would have laughed quietly to myself. I knew certainly that I was not, and if pregnancy was like this, then I'm afraid the species would die out. It was funny to realize that everyone besides my family thought I was probably over-dramatizing. I probably *should* have been at the hospital getting fluids through an I.V. and canceling the concert, but every time I wanted to give in I thought of the kids needing scholarships. I decided it didn't matter what anyone thought. Besides, what was I looking for, applause? Nevertheless, I probably should have joined in on the bet. I'm not the betting kind of girl, but I had an inside tip....

I don't know how much time had passed, but at some point my family came in and said it was about time for the concert to start. I groaned. The moment was coming when I would have to walk out onstage. The last thing we do before we take our places offstage, just beyond the lights and the curtains, is say a prayer. I honestly can't remember who said the prayer, but I remember someone's voice pleading on my behalf, praying that we could bless the lives of the students needing scholarships. They prayed that I would play as though I were healthy.

Next thing I knew, my arms were over the shoulders of Bryan and my mom, and they were buoying me up the stairs to take my place alongside my siblings offstage. I could hear the announcement—"PLACES!"—over the backstage speakers as I stumbled along.

My siblings were already in place when I joined them. They gave me sympathetic looks and stayed silent rather than pity me with words. I understood they felt bad even asking this of me, and I felt their gratitude to me for at least trying. I crouched on the ground while they stood and waited for the cue. I could see the lights set onstage and hear the roar of the crowd as their cumulative chatter rose en masse.

Then the cue came. The moment, the impossible moment I had been dreading, was here, and the reality of the moment deafened my ears. The high dive, the high dive, I was thinking…. I could feel the sun on my face, the wind whipping my wispy childlike hair across my cheeks, as I stared hypnotized by the shiny rippling water below. My family, distant, were silently mouthing words of encouragement…then, with the lights dimming and the audience's murmuring faded to silence, Bryan helped lift me to my feet. I stood, looking from the comforting darkness just beyond the stage lights out onto the brilliantly lit stage and then…jumped into the unknown. With that first step onto the stage it felt as though my body were a garment of clothing being lifted off the bed by the hanger. Suddenly I was standing erect, with the pain and sickness in my stomach gone. It felt like I was flying, gliding across the stage to join my brothers and sisters, who were standing beside their pianos waiting for me. The audience was roaring with applause and cheers. Once I took my position, the cue was given, and we all bowed in sync. Then we took our places at the pianos and Deondra made eye contact with each one of us to know when to start. She paused when she came to me and did a little nod with an eyebrow slightly raised. I nodded back. She gave me a small, determined smile, which I returned, and started into the first strains of *Rhapsody in Blue* by George Gershwin.

   I think I played with a devotion I had never felt so intensely before. I had something to give. I had been given so much that I would give back to the best of my ability. Like the kids waiting to know if they would be receiving scholarships, I too had dreamed of a life beyond the one I knew. I had grown up in a small town where having dreams of going to New York City to follow a passion was a little weird. I was a girl with a few too many opinions and a dream maybe too big. I read insatiably of people going to far off places and living unimaginable lives. I listened to recordings of legendary women pianists like Martha Argerich, Alicia de Larrocha, and the Labèque Sisters, and dreamed of being like them. I read and reread probably a hundred times a BBC music magazine featuring the Labèque Sisters, a French two-piano team that I likened to Deondra and myself. As a kid I would set the magazine on the piano to inspire me while I practiced. Deep inside me there was a truth lurking: the knowledge that if I worked hard enough, I could be like them. It frightened me how real that truth was. It meant that I too would need to go to far-off places to work and pursue the unknown.

And here I was, sick on a stage in Knoxville, Tennessee, but still, living a dream. I knew this as I played and was grateful. I played with all my heart. At different points in the performance I saw my siblings look at me in surprise and amazement. How could I explain that my heart was so full? They would look, and then dedicate themselves even more to their own playing. I think they understood. Melody and I locked eyes for a moment near the end of the final piece of the concert, *The Firebird* by Igor Stravinsky. There is a moment almost near the end of the piece when the final chordal strains of two pianos are playing over the rumblings of the other three pianos. She looked at me there with glistening eyes and a serious smile as she threw herself into those triumphant chords. We understood that miracles happen, and that we were living one.

As the five of us finished *The Firebird*, we walked around the pianos to the very front of the stage as the audience rose to their feet. Standing in a row, we took each other's hands and, Broadway-style, raised them above our heads and then swung down for a deep bow. Then, smiling, we walked off the stage.

Once I was in the darkness offstage, I ran for the trashcan and was sick again. My brothers and sisters looked at me, confused, and then walked back onstage without me to take the rest of the bows. My miracle was over, but yet again in my life, the impossible had become real.

Bryan walked me down to the green room where I fell, exhausted, into the sofa. I lay there and closed my eyes as he stroked my head. I did not sleep, though. I offered a prayer of gratitude for the opportunity to have been made an instrument in the hands of God.

I hear that the students who couldn't afford college went on to be music majors as a result of the concert we played. Some time has passed since that performance, and they are probably halfway done getting their degrees. By the time you read this they may have graduated or gone off living their own dreams somewhere. They will probably never realize that a small miracle contributed to the realization of at least one of those dreams. It makes me think of all the miracles that I may not be aware of in my own life, and I feel grateful.

Oh, and old Bob, James, and Wilkins lost their bet. We *did* come back to Tennessee and play again, but there was no mini-me. The stagehands laughed and a little shamefacedly admitted to making the bet. Apparently, everyone backstage was in on it.

* * *

As I closed the door I felt relieved for a second to be out of the cab, until I saw the ancient furniture shop again. The place looked like it was going to collapse just from me walking through the front door. I paused when I saw a suspicious-looking man at the front desk. "I'm Ryan Brown...," I said. It felt like a question. "Is this the right place?"

DIRTY, SECRET PEOPLE

BY RYAN BROWN

New York City
Summer 2005

Heavy eyes, bobbing heads, and, well, some drool—if you're Greg—are three common things that take place five minutes into driving to the oh-so-common airport. The three of us tried to get an uncomfortable ounce of sleep in the hot car after a long day of school, practicing, and packing. We were suddenly awakened by what seemed to be an overly loud cell phone ring.

"Oh, hi, Dad," Melody said in a sleepy voice.

"Did you get everything before you left your apartment? Concert clothes, music, and your passport?" asked Dad.

"Yes, Dad, I did," Melody replied.

"Did Gregory and Ryan get all those things as well?"

"Yeah, I think so," Melody said, looking at Gregory and me, as though we heard every word Dad had said through the little earpiece on her junky little phone.

"Okay, but are you sure you got your passports?"

"Yes, yes we did! Ryan is actually showing me, right now, his dumb little picture that was taken years ago," Melody answered, making me think, *Gosh, what happened to me? I looked so much cuter as a twelve-year-old.*

Dad laughed. "All right, I believe you. Our flight is just about to take off over here in Salt Lake, so we'll talk to you guys when you get into England! Love you and hope you have a great flight!"

"Okay, Dad, we will. Love you too, and we'll talk to you soon."

Forty-five minutes later, with sweaty backs and "evening breath," we finally reached our destination. We hit the airport after what seemed to be the longest drive ever because of the New York City rush hour. We pulled ourselves and our bags out of the car and strolled into the Delta terminal. Luggage rolling over the airport floor never seemed so loud. Just the three of us sounded like a marching army, distracting others as we walked to the ticket counter. The woman kindly asked us where we were flying.

"England," Greg replied.

"Oh yes, the computer shows all of you on the flight." Smiling, she asked, "May I have your passports?" We handed them to her.

She looked at Greg's first and printed out his ticket. "You're all set, have a great flight!" she said.

"Thanks," he replied, and waited for the woman to check in Melody and me.

Next, she looked at Melody's passport, printed out her ticket, and said, "You're all set as well, and have a great flight!"

"Thank you," Melody said.

Then I stepped forward. The woman picked up my passport, opened it and said, as though she were talking to a five-year-old, "Aw, you look so cute in this picture!" Even though I still looked very young, I had just turned eighteen two months ago and wanted to be treated like an adult. I knew that was unlikely because I was always going to look fifteen years old one way or another for the rest of my life.

As the woman looked at me, waiting for some kind of response to her little compliment, doing anything but making eye contact seemed the obvious choice. Nevertheless, I still smiled and chuckled as my face turned bright red. The woman, still smiling, continued looking over my passport. Then all of a sudden her smile left and she looked concerned.

"It seems as though your passport expired two months ago. How old are you?"

I replied quickly, "I turned eighteen two months ago!"

"Oh, no. Your passport must have expired when you turned eighteen."

Panic. Our flight left in one hour, and the concert was in forty-eight hours! The three of us pleaded with her to see if she would let me fly to England, and because she was so nice, she said she would. She then mentioned that trying to get back home from England would be the big problem. "You could be stuck in Europe for who knows how long if I let you go," she explained.

I panicked thinking about getting old and gray in England. We tried calling everyone we could to get some direction on what we should do. First we thought of our family, but then we remembered that they were all on the plane with Dad headed to England. So we thought quickly about whom to call next.

"Our record label!" Melody called out. So we all looked in our cell phones and started calling all the people we knew at our record label. We couldn't reach anybody at the office. Being on our phones for thirty minutes seemed to be getting us nowhere. It was after hours, and nobody was picking up the phone. We wondered if calling any relatives could help us make any progress. We decided to call our Aunt Nikki—a stylist who tried to help us look way better for our music videos than we normally did—who may have had connections with the record label. When we called, she actually picked up her phone. She was the only person who did after we tried calling twenty people!

"Nikki, hi, this is Greg! We have an emergency and we were wondering if you had anybody's number over at the record label!"

"I don't!" Nikki explained, disappointed. "The only number I have is the producer of the music video you guys did a few months ago."

"I don't know if his number will help us at all, but we'll take it just in case," said Greg. "Anyway, thanks so much Nikki, and we'll let you know how it goes."

We stopped to think about what our options were, and we felt that we had no choice but to call that producer guy. "Hi, Bill, this is Greg Brown.... I know you're a busy guy, and I'm sorry to bother you, but we have an emergency at the airport and need to talk to anybody we can at the record company. Do you have anybody's cell phone number?"

"Looks like I have Karen's cell phone number—will that help?" Bill asked.

"Yes," Greg sounded grateful. "Thank you so much, Bill. You're a lifesaver! Oh, and sorry again about the strange urgent call. Have a good night producing videos! You're a genius!"

Greg hung up and called out, "Yes! We got Karen's cell phone number." Karen happened to be the record company's main assistant. As we were just about to call her, we heard over the intercom that our flight had ten minutes before takeoff. Greg hurriedly dialed Karen, and she actually picked up.

"Hello?"

"Hi, Karen, this is Greg Brown." Greg's composure went out the window as he explained our little crisis.

"Oh, no!" She paused for a second. The tone in her voice changed from urgent to calm and in control. "I'll take care of it. You and Melody go ahead to England, and Ryan and I will work things out. Don't worry about a thing. We'll get him there."

Unconvinced, Greg said, "Really? Don't passports usually take months to complete?"

"Don't worry about a thing, everything will be just fine."

Still skeptical, Greg responded, "Okay.... Thanks, Karen, for taking care of things. We owe you one."

As Greg and Melody started making their way to the security checkpoint, Melody turned and said, "You going to be okay, Ryan?"

I replied, with a half-smirk on my face, "We'll see! Hopefully." I shrugged. I felt so alone and confused about what to do and where to go as they walked away. I thought, "Karen's got me taken care of…at least she says so…but you know, what does that even mean? It takes months to receive a passport! How is this possible? Oh, well…we'll see what happens tomorrow."

I was in the cab going back to our New York apartment when Karen called. "Do you have a pen and paper? I have some things I need you to write down," she said.

"Um, okay," I replied. What I really thought as I scrambled for a pen was, "Who does she think I am, some nerd who just whips out a pen and paper from my geeky pocket-protector or fanny-pack?" I asked her to hold on a second while I looked in my wallet for a piece of paper. The only one I could find had the number of a girl I never called. I started getting distracted. That girl was cute, and I should have asked her out. Karen then started listing off some directions, and I snapped back to reality. She was giving me crazy directions to some place downtown that I'd never heard of. I was a little surprised I didn't know it, having lived in New York City for over four years. "Meet me there at five o'clock in the morning. Oh, and somehow I need to get a copy of your birth certificate," she said.

"You got it, Karen, whatever you say." I thought it would be better if I didn't ask questions, but what I really wanted to say was, "Where on earth are we going, Karen!? And why the heck do I have to get up at stinkin' five in the morning to get there!" I decided that if I said that, I would have sounded a little too much like my sisters when they get tired and overreact, so I kept it to myself.

I woke up the next morning feeling like I was still in the same nightmare I was at the airport. I tried to make myself look nice as best I could at five in the morning, because I knew I would probably have to take a new passport photo. You know, you've got to at least try to have a good passport picture. I had a lot to live up to because of the cutesy little picture on my expired passport. I didn't even have to try to look cute back then. Now I was all old and busted, but I wanted to keep up the trend with the ladies at the airport desks saying I looked cute.

After I was done trying to look like I was ready for the impending photo shoot, I got on the subway with what seemed to be only homeless people. Sitting there looking all preppy with the homeless people staring at me, I started to kick myself for forgetting to do my nightly pushups just in case any of them decided to jump me for all I'm worth. I was outnumbered about ten to one, and I was itching to get off. When the subway car got to the right stop I was relieved that I could still feel my wallet in my back pocket.

As I walked down the street to the odd location, the city still seemed asleep. It was unusually quiet even for five-thirty in the morning. I stopped on a street corner, hoping this was where Karen had told me to meet her. She showed up just five minutes later, cheerful and happy. How can someone have so much energy at such an early hour, especially knowing what all had to be done that day? Was it the coffee? Because I personally felt like, well, not so good. Karen asked me cheerfully, "Did you get your birth certificate?"

"Yup. Had it faxed in by my brother-in-law last night." I had no idea why I needed it. Then she said, "Okay, you need to wait outside, while I take care of this upstairs."

She went into this mystery building for about an hour while I waited outside freezing to death because I'd decided I was tough this morning and didn't need a jacket. After the long wait, she came out all happy again, like this was some kind of game or adventure. Again, I didn't ask any questions because I felt like it wasn't my place, and I got the feeling that she didn't want to disclose any information about what was going on. I kept my mouth shut, yet again.

Then we got in a cab and drove for quite a long time. For once she actually told me where we were going. She said we were going to a "passport place." Even though that's all she said, I was still happy because it was the most information I had gotten since the whole predicament began the night before. When we arrived at the "passport place," we took an elevator upstairs to this vast floor in what seemed to be the biggest "passport place" on the earth. We walked past the crowd of people in line like we were celebrities. We went to a back area where there stood one man. Karen walked up to him and started talking secretively. I was confused because she was whispering to him only five feet away from me. I just acted like I couldn't hear anything, even though I caught a word here and there. From what little I heard, it sounded like a lot of pressure was being put on this guy to do something, but I couldn't really catch what it was. I could tell that the guy was looking at me thinking, or hoping, that I was somebody important. I got the feeling he didn't like me much, but I didn't care because it was mutual. After he looked at me for a second, he said, "Hey, you look like Prince Harry!"

Oh, great, I thought. *Not this again. Why do people say that? Prince Harry is cool, and you know, I'm just kind of not.* After the man said I looked like Prince Harry, he started acting more urgent and involved. Karen and the man talked a bit more, and then he just disappeared. Karen came up to me and started asking me hundreds of questions about things I barely knew the answers to—questions about family history, social security numbers, places where I've lived, and information about my parents. I felt like my answers were educated guesses, but she seemed to think what I was giving her could work. I didn't know if Karen wanted the information to procure a passport or what. It seemed as though the whole thing was a crazy, classified FBI operation. After I was done telling Karen what I knew, she disappeared for fifteen minutes, then came back and said, "Okay, there's another place I need you to go. Here are the directions. Oh, and they're waiting for you. I need to take care of more stuff while you're gone, so good luck and I'll see you soon." I felt as though I was going undercover or something. I mean, "They're waiting for you" and "good luck"? I'd had a very confusing day, but this topped everything.

I left the "passport place," got a cab, and told the driver where I needed to go. He looked back at me, and with a thick New York accent demanded, "What? *Where?*" I repeated the address. He shrugged and said, "Okay...."

I thought, *Oh, man. Who is this guy? Is he really a cab driver? He doesn't even know the address! This is not good.*

It was already 1 p.m., and my flight to England left in three hours. The cab driver said the place should be coming up on the left. "Where did you say this address was again?" he asked. I told him for the third time, and he said, "Yeah, I think this is it!"

I was confused. "Are you sure? It looks like an old furniture store."

"What are you looking for, kid?"

"I'm not sure, possibly some passport place?" Now he looked at me like I was crazy. I didn't even know where I was going, and we had parked outside some nineteenth-century furniture shop. I got the feeling he wanted me out of his cab, so I hopped out in a rush so I wouldn't get in a fight with him. I could tell he didn't like me much. Let me tell ya, you never want to fight with a cab driver. They will really jack you up. I once saw a fight between two cab drivers, and it got real ugly, real fast. If things got ugly between this cab driver and me, I wouldn't have a chance. He was huge and tough. I swear, he probably bench-pressed his car for exercise; he was that big. As I closed the door I felt relieved for a second to be out of the cab, until I saw the ancient furniture shop again. The place looked like it was going to collapse just from me walking through the front door. I paused when I saw a suspicious-looking man at the front desk. "I'm Ryan Brown...," I said. It felt like a question. "Is this the right place?"

"Yes, it is. Come with me." I wasn't sure if I should feel awesome for finding the right place, or feel more awesome because I was being treated like some kind of secret agent; everything was so secretive. He escorted me to the back of the shop, where there was a chair on the ground with a blanket behind it. Turned out he wanted to take a passport photo, but I couldn't figure it out—why would Karen send me all the way down here to get a passport photo? Why didn't they take one at the last place? By now I started worrying that I would miss my flight. If I missed this one, I would miss our first performance in England. And the press! I had forgotten that a lot of international press would be at that performance. If one of The 5 Browns is missing, none of our five-piano pieces work. This could be a catastrophe.

I got two prints—one big and one small. They only took one picture, though, and after I saw it I wanted to ask for another one, because by this time my hair was messed up, my clothes were wrinkled, and my face was red and greasy from the heat and teenage acne. I looked like a mess, and my smile—oh, you should have seen my smile. It was awful. I looked like I was in pain and laughing about it. Now, instead of the ladies at the airport counters telling me I looked cute, they would ask, "Is this you? You don't look so good."

Anyway, I had to get out of there. Karen had called again telling me to meet her at yet another location. She gave me some hope, though. She said it was the last place I needed to go. All my energy returned when I heard that the end was near. When I met her at this last location I gave her the two ugly photos, and she looked at them and chuckled. "I know, I know," I said, "laugh all you want." She disappeared yet again, and I didn't see her for another thirty minutes. When she returned, she had a big grin on her face. In her hand she held a beautiful blue passport.

As she walked toward me I said, "No, it can't be. You got it?"

"Yep! Take a look!"

I looked at it for a second and saw something I didn't think I should be seeing. "Is it...," I paused, "Is it supposed to say Ryan *Browm*? There's, um, an *M* at the end."

"What?" she snatched the passport from my hand. "Oh, no, we have to fix this. We have fifteen minutes before you need to get in a cab to the airport." She ran back inside. Exactly *sixteen* minutes later, Karen came running out with the passport in her hands, crying, "We've got it! We need to get you out of here *now*!"

We started urgently looking for a cab and couldn't spot one for the longest time, making this the longest part of my crazy day. The three minutes it took to hail a cab seemed like three hours. Once in the cab I rolled down the window and yelled, "Thanks so much, Karen! I can't believe you got it! I totally owe you one...or something!"

Sitting on the airplane on my way to England, I began to reflect—the unknown can actually be kind of fun. Especially if you don't know why you're traveling, walking, and waiting in those strange places to begin with. Turns out, I barely made it to the performance in England on time, showing up five minutes before I was supposed to be onstage.

Does it really take all the mystery, questions, strange places, and, well…dirty, secret people to get a passport in ten hours? If you ask me, without the dirty, secret people, nothing would have been possible.

* * *

"...Because I know a guy, and I'm gonna hire him to cut off every one of your little piano-playing fingers—one by one!"
—Romeo, from atop a car in the middle of Broadway

ROMEO AND LANCE

BY GREGORY BROWN

The Juilliard Dormitory
New York City
February 2001

Okay, so even though the thought of a hand-hitman is quite the unsavory and gruesome one—especially for a pianist—the more I think about the touching tableau above, the more I begin to see that these very well could be the most romantic words I've ever heard one dude utter to another. Before you go thinking I've got serious issues, I should offer a little analysis of our Broadway Romeo's passionate spectacle. Take the first part, for instance: "Because I know a guy, and I'm gonna hire him." This is actually a simple plea of self-worth from a desperate man in love—in other words: "don't leave me; I have tons of really fun friends and a lot of money." The second part is even more endearing: "to cut off every one of your little piano-playing fingers." It seems clear now that this means nothing other than "I love you so much; it's absolutely *painful* for you to leave me like this." When you look at it like that, it's actually kind of sweet, right? And the whole "one-by-one" part? Merely a reaffirmation of endless devotion.

Yes, the dude was standing on a car, and yes, he was yelling incoherent threats about torture and dismemberment, but thankfully, these sweet nothings weren't directed my way. I was merely an innocent bystander. They were actually intended for one of my good friends from Juilliard, whom, for lack of a better pseudonym, we'll just go ahead and call Lance. But before I get into how I ended up on the corner of 66th and Broadway with Romeo and Lance, let me step back in time just a bit.

Juilliard has what they call a Pre-College division for twerpy little runts who enjoy being tortured but aren't yet old enough for college. Melody, Ryan, and I joined the ranks of this genius-in-training program, complete with hundreds of psychotic stage parents, surreptitious practice-room romances, and enough acne to result in lifetimes of psychotherapy (I'm speaking from personal experience, of course). We began attending this division a year after our older sisters got into Juilliard's college program, and my parents actually moved from Utah to New York in order for us to do so.

On starting school there, I soon met and befriended Lance. He was one of those little balls of energy that never stop jumping off of things and testing your patience, but he was also one of the most insanely talented pianists I had ever known in my life. He sort of reminded me of a Chihuahua or a Capri Sun, where the unbelievable inner awesomeness plus the tiny packaging equals a frustrating mismatch. But he was a way funny kid, so just as I'll forever be a consumer of the heavenly fruit punch in silver mini-pouches despite their annoyingly small size, Lance and I became good friends. The kid was maybe five foot three, and I was already over six feet at the time, so I'd go out on a limb and say there probably wasn't a more wicked-awesome Mormon-Jew duo on the planet—provided Donny Osmond and Barry Manilow never join forces to thrill the world, that is.

Lance was a blast to hang out with, and we used to walk around the school talking about the one girl we thought was so cute and wished we had the nerve to ask out. (The Pre-College student body included only one mildly attractive girl.) These were the years when Lance and I batted on the same team—before he stepped across the plate, of course. He and I had been huge fans of the visiting team for years, but he finally came to the conclusion that the home team had cuter outfits. This happened around the time that we both got into Juilliard's college program, and it was fine by me, because it drastically diminished my competition for the almost-hot girl. Coming from a small town in Utah, I hadn't known many gay guys in my young life, but he was still my good friend, and the two of us continued to hang out quite a bit.

As Lance quickly rose to the stature of starting shortstop for the home team, his brand-new freedom was sadly accompanied by an urge to go overboard with experimentation in almost every way. He soon found himself in a scene that was not entirely the safest place for little seventeen-year-old freshmen, or anyone for that matter—a completely illegal scene that undoubtedly included the likes of Dennis Rodman and the nasty old businessmen you see on *To Catch a Predator* who make you cheer when the cops rough 'em up real good.

With this newfound scene, complete with partying and substance abuse, I began to see less and less of my favorite pint-sized friend as freshman year rolled on. He started dating some Norman Bates guy he had met over the Internet, a guy the rest of his Juilliard friends and I regarded with skepticism, to say the least. The guy's online profile was way creepy and overtly slimy, and you'd think that might've been enough to set off warning bells in Lance's head, but he insisted that Norman was a really sweet man (I say *man* because he was probably old enough to be Lance's father). The rest of my friends were also pretty worried for Lance's physical safety—not to mention his grades—because he would regularly come back to the dorms with cuts and big, colorful bruises all over. When it came to his music, everything that he had worked so hard for was beginning to slip through his fingers, and playing the piano quickly began to take a back seat to all-night drag parties, Jack Daniels, and bankruptcy at Bloomingdale's.

Back to our beautiful nighttime tableau on 66th and Broadway. It was near the end of our freshman year, and I was practicing in my pajamas in one of the dorm building's practice rooms just before bed. As I was dozing off at the piano in this cozy little six-by-six padded cell, Lance comes bursting through the door with tears in his eyes. He said that Norman (aka Romeo) had been hitting and abusing him, that he was trying to leave Romeo, but Romeo wouldn't have it. He wasn't sure how to get out of the relationship without being further abused, and asked if I'd help him. Of course I said I would, and I thought maybe he'd want me to make an angry phone call to Romeo or leave a flaming brown bag on his doorstep or something, but there was no way I could've been prepared for what he actually had in mind. "I want you to be my bodyguard," he said.

Okay, now hold up. Let's take some time to draw you a nice mental picture of my physique during freshman year. Try imagining a stunning, perfectly proportioned Ken doll made out of Play-Doh. Now, take Ken—a replica of the ideal male body type—and stretch him out so that he's about twice as long as he originally was. Now, pull on his arms until they reach three quarters of his overall height, and roll them with your fingers until they're about the width of toothpicks. After you've done the same with his legs, be sure to cut off his butt and pectorals until a view from the side is something similar to that of a two-by-four. Now step on his feet and find a Barbie whose hair is in knots. Remove that nest from her head and put it on Ken's, and there you have it, ladies and gentleman—Greg Brown!

So obviously, my first instinct was to laugh at the poor kid when he asked me to be his bodyguard. I mean, let's face it, how could I possibly be anything other than a liability in this situation? My second instinct, however, was to run away and hide someplace, because after hearing stories about this Romeo guy, the thought of going through with it was actually terrifying. I had never been in a real fight before, and

Romeo sounded like a total freak. What if I had to actually fight him or something? I would probably be torn limb from limb—maybe even killed! Okay, I'll admit that may be a bit over the top, but still, I was such a wimp that the thought actually did cross my mind. I mean, my arms are pretty long, so maybe I *could* get the first punch in, but that would just buy me enough time to run away as fast as possible. But how could I even consider saying no to poor, teary-eyed Lance? He was my good friend, and he needed my help, so grudgingly I said I'd do it.

"Okay, I guess I could do it, but what exactly do you need me to do?" I asked.

"Oh, you just have to come downstairs with me right now and help me get some of my stuff back. It's in his car, but he won't let me have it back because he refuses to let me go." With that, I'm nearly positive my pants turned into the blacktop on pit row during the Indy 500. He was here? I had to do this *now*?

"But I'm in my p.j.'s, and we both know I look really skinny in my p.j.'s. There's no way he'd be intimidated by me," I whined. So he suggested we look through my closet to see what we could find that seemed even slightly threatening. Unfortunately, there wasn't much there to fit the bill, so we turned instead to my roommate's side of the room. Now, my assigned roomie at the time also happened to bat for the opposite team. He was definitely more beefy and muscular than I was, which meant that his clothes would likely be a bit bulkier. Sorting through dress shirt after stylish colorful dress shirt, we finally stumbled upon a big, puffy winter coat that would have to do. I threw it on, and we walked out the door.

We hurried out of the dorm building and down to the street, and that's when I saw Romeo for the first time. He had parked his car in a no-parking zone in the middle of Broadway and was sitting on its hood, twiddling his thumbs with a giant scowl on his face. He was a heck of a lot older than I expected, and he wasn't a total giant, so my fears subsided a bit. When he saw Lance and me approaching, his face started twitching all funny-like, and it became pretty obvious that this guy was every bit as psycho as his reputation. He looked antsy and ready to explode from the slightest provocation, so whatever hope I had gleaned from his stature was all but erased because he wasn't in a straitjacket.

At this point I began to be incredibly aware of my appearance—probably because I wasn't the only one aware of it at the moment. I had been so consumed by finding something that would make my muscles look massive that I had completely neglected to consider the ensemble as a whole—which, needless to say, resulted in me looking anything but fearsome.

Let's start from the bottom, beginning with the feet, and work our way up. At this point in my life, I was on this stupid no-shoes-at-any-time kick. I purchased these ridiculous Adidas sports sandals, so popular a decade ago, and decided that they were so insanely cool that they had to be worn everywhere I went. Come rain, come snow, come summer, come winter (which season it now was), I could always be found in those amazing sandals. They were kind of like my trademark. Next, we have my pajama pants. These darling maroon medical scrubs I bought a few years before my final growth spurt, so they were two inches too short, exposing a thin tuft of scrappy hair growing on an emaciated ankle. They were fairly formfitting on the legs, but seeing as though our Ken doll had had his gluteus minimus-es savagely shorn, there was considerable space in the back. I'm sure you've all seen those toddlers with tight pajama pants and a sagging, dirty diaper falling off in back; well, that's pretty close to what we're dealing with here. Above the pants, of course, we have our puffy, designer winter coat—an item obviously purchased by a very gay man. ("OMG, that coat is *so* fabulous" were Lance's words on our way downstairs.) The problem with this coat, however, was my gangly arms. It was undoubtedly made for men who weren't born with apelike deformities, so the sleeves were way too short on me. Again, they exposed dainty, naked wrists that complemented my bulging new façade rather famously. Finally, we have my head. My hair wasn't fixed that day, and *that* wasn't gonna look very good in public, so I threw on my favorite Texas Longhorns cap and felt pretty good about sidestepping a near mishap. Okay, so zoom back out and take a look at me from top to bottom. A burnt orange cap, a cropped and stylish puffy white coat, ill-fitting maroon scrubs, and black Adidas sports sandals—or in other words, straight, gay, faux pas, and are you kidding. Contrast this with the perfectly coordinated and glamorous attire of my current homosexual company, and that pretty much explains the look on Romeo's face when he saw me.

We walked up to him, but he didn't notice my presence at first. He just glared at Lance.

"I want my stuff back," Lance sassed.

"Not a chance. You'll have to go through me to get it," Romeo snapped. The two of them started going at it, and finally Lance just walked over to the car and began trying to reclaim his stuff. At this, Romeo rushed over to stop him, and against my better judgment, I slid in between the two of them.

"Who is this?" Romeo was taken off guard.

"Maybe he's my new boyfriend," Lance said snidely. Right about now is when my pants went from pit-lane tarmac to the ground beneath the starting gate at the Kentucky Derby. For what seemed like an eternity, Romeo eyeballed me up and down, obviously hypnotized by the train wreck enveloping my body. Then at last:

"I'm absolutely loving this coat," he said, after which he began to laugh at his own diva wit. "Do you really expect me to believe that *this* is your boyfriend?"

I was determined not to say a word and decided that a good strategy would be to just stand there looking as menacing as possible. Romeo actually looked a little thrown off his game by me, and he seemed not quite to know what to do. I think this had more to do with me looking like some angry deaf-mute who had just escaped a mental institution and stolen whatever clothes he could get his hands on, rather than actually intimidating him, but whatever it was, it seemed to do the trick. His confusion bought Lance just enough time to finish grabbing his stuff out of the car, and after he finished, the two of us backed up and began to leave.

Romeo finally came back to his senses, noticed that Lance had reclaimed all of his stuff while he had stood there mesmerized by the dumb bodyguard, and then the stink really hit the fan. He started yelling curses left and right and banging on the hood of his car with his fist. He even made like he was gonna attack Lance, but another glimpse of the top-heavy marshmallow on two maroon ski poles seemed to again stop him dead in his tracks. Instead he turned around, dejected, and walked back to his car. Just as he was about to get in and drive away, he apparently thought better of it, slammed the car door, climbed on top of the roof, and the barbaric display that followed is for the history books.

In the time it takes for an angry pedophile in fabulous Gucci shoes to climb off of a luxury vehicle, Lance and I made a quick getaway. We took off, the threats of dismemberment and carnage fainter and fainter behind us, and at last, we were home free. Returning to the dorms, we exulted in the unlikely success of the heist, far too elated to deprive ourselves of an epic celebration.

"What should we do now?" I asked as we engaged in a jumping hug for the ages (the jumping hug is the greatest of all hugs).

"How about we find all of my pictures of him and cut them up?" he said. This was by far the best thing I had heard all night. I had always seen people cutting up pictures of ex-

lovers in the movies but had never disliked anyone enough to take part in such a satisfying vent. After finding every possible photo, we went back to my padded cell—he sitting on the piano, and I on the bench—and we gave Romeo a little taste of his own medicine. We laughed as we chopped off heads and sang songs of victory as we lopped off arms. But suddenly it was like the record stopped. Out from the stack of pictures slipped a rather suggestive one that was definitely not for my eyes.

"You know, I think I've probably had enough for tonight," I said. "Maybe you should finish this up without me."

To redeem himself from being the killjoy and scarring my so-called pure and innocent Mormon mind, Lance quickly suggested, "How about we burn them instead? Then we don't have to look at them."

My spirits instantly soared at the prospect of emancipating my inner pyro. Everyone knows that the only thing better than burning leaves with a magnifying glass as a kid is burning real stuff with actual fire.

"But how could we possibly make a bonfire in a dorm room in the middle of New York City without getting in huge trouble?" I asked. The two of us racked our brains. After a few moments Lance said:

"I've got it! Follow me."

We went back to his room, where he grabbed his roommate's little plastic trashcan and began stuffing it with all the old pictures.

I grinned. "Brilliant!"

"And while we're at it, why don't we add a few other things," he continued, throwing in some old ticket stubs, a mix CD, and a cute little teddy bear that sang "Dancing Queen" by Abba. Trashcan of fuel and box of matches in hand, we ran out the door and down the stairwell. It was obvious to us both what the next step was.

We stopped at the door to the seventeenth floor. This was the quiet floor, where all the losers who went to bed at nine lived, and we knew that it was the only place where everyone would definitely be asleep already. We quietly opened the door to suite 1701, stepped into the bathroom, and locked ourselves in. Trying our hardest to stifle laughter, and failing half the time, we opened the curtain to one of the shower stalls and set the little trashcan on the drain. Both of us lit a match, tossed it onto the stack of pictures, and waited. At first, nothing happened, but just as we were about to throw a couple more matches in, it was as though someone had recently doused that poor little teddy bear with lighter fluid. The whole thing went up in giant flames. High-fives were a-flyin' as Lance and I watched the remains of his relationship incinerate in the most glorious bonfire Juilliard's ever seen. As we were at the peak of our celebration, that dang teddy bear really started picking up, and the flames were going to town on him like you wouldn't believe.

We started getting a bit apprehensive about our giant shower fire, and the room was filling up with smoke pretty fast. Just then, Satan Bear started making the freakiest sounds I've ever heard. I swear, it was moaning "Dancing Queen" an octave too low and in slow motion as flames shot out of its eyeballs. Even though it was one of the funniest things I'd ever seen, mixed with the thick smoke and flames the scene spooked us pretty good. We threw the shower water on, opened the door, and ran the heck outta there. Possessed Teddy's psycho requiem trailed us out the door as we sprinted back up to my room, slammed the door, and bolted it twice. I don't remember laughing that hard my entire freshman year. To this day, I can't hear "Dancing Queen" without seeing that demented little bear's face staring at me like one of the melting Nazis at the end of *Raiders of the Lost Ark*. It was a victory for the ages.

Lance had his stuff back, the photos were gone, and Teddy Queen had been "taken care of," but as we came running back up those stairs to my suite, Lance and I came back down to earth again. After standing there for a few seconds, Lance finally looked up at me with tears building in his eyes.

"Greg, I've got nowhere to go."

He had been kicked out of the dorms for substance abuse and was living out of his suitcase at Romeo's place. For some reason, I had completely forgotten this, and the reality of it obviously pained him more than the bruises his shirtsleeve couldn't quite conceal. He had no home, he had lost most of his real friends, he was failing all of his classes, he wasn't on speaking terms with his family, and he hadn't even touched a piano in over a month. I knew the kid needed help, and even though he and I had walked separate paths for most of the year, he was still my friend, and it was apparent that he had nowhere else to turn.

"I'll go with you tomorrow, and we can appeal to the dorm advisor. I bet they'll let you back in within a day or two.

Until then, if it's not too uncomfortable, why don't you just crash on my floor for now."

As he pulled his blanket up to his chin, I peered down over my bunk-rail to say good night.

"Could we keep the closet light on, Greg? It always makes me feel a little better."

"Sure, bud, not a problem. I'm so tired right now, I probably won't even notice." My eyes were drifting into sleep.

"…You know, Greg? I think maybe I'll do a little practicing tomorrow…."

* * *

There are only a handful of decisions in life that are so important your entire future hinges upon them. Each is often accompanied by great turmoil and uncertainty. The most important decision of all is directly in front of me. The magnitude of a few key choices will singlehandedly change the course of my life forever.

AN UNCONVENTIONAL PATH

BY DEONDRA BROWN

New York City
December 2002

"I think we're not supposed to be together," I sputtered out through frantic tears. As difficult as the words were to form on my lips, the second they came out they felt right. As tears streamed down my face, the reality of what I was saying began to take hold. He was speechless. I had no solid reason to give him, and yet I was certain it needed to be said. A huge, gaping hole began to form in my heart.

I knew this decision was right, but that didn't make it any easier. I felt numb and yet pained at the same time. It was the hardest thing I had ever done—ending a perfectly good relationship, for no reason other than a gut feeling. I had been seeking divine wisdom, inspiration as to whether this guy was the right one for me—and when I least expected it, the answer to my prayers had come. As clear as day, there it was. The impact was monumental, and the repercussions unfathomable.

And of course, it was just before the holidays. The thought of spending this time of year alone *again* was almost unbearable. It's amazing how one can be in a house full of people and still feel alone. But along with Christmas break would come a much-needed escape from *everything*. I welcomed the opportunity to go home and regroup up in the peaceful mountains of Utah, away from the craziness of relationships and college life that is New York City. It would be a real chance to get my head together and make sense of all that had happened.

Although the break-up was still fresh, I was determined to move forward instead of backward. Any communication between us caused me to sink back into despair, and so after one brief slip, I vowed never to look back. I have never been one to change my mind after making a decision, and this would be no different. No dwelling on the past, and no second-guessing. And besides, my answer was so complete there was no need for turning back.

The beauty and comforts of home brought me, mostly, back to my normal self. The mourning period was all but over, and I was beginning to grow more comfortable with my singleness again. Happiness could only be right around the corner. Before I knew it, most of the holiday season had passed, and New Year's Eve was upon us. It's a tradition in our family to drive to one of the nicest restaurants in the area, which has a fabulous view of the city, and have dinner while we watch the sunset. This year was no different. The roster was the same—my parents, two brothers and two sisters, brother-in-law Bryan, and me—forever solo. All eight of us packed into the family Suburban, each attempt over the years steadily becoming more and more difficult. We definitely weren't kids anymore. It was squishy with all of us, but we wouldn't have it any other way (until we realized we had a whole forty-five-minute trip ahead of us this way).

With Gregory all but sitting in my lap, it began: the constant and ever-changing conversation that has come to make Brown holidays (and family outings in general) legendary. It's open season for anything and everything.

Gregory: "Hey, Deon, I bet you wish it was Chuck crammed here next to you instead of me, huh?"

Me: "At least he would have had better breath.... Smells like you just drank from the toilet, dude."

Gregory: "Why, thank you! Seriously though, no offense, but I'm totally relieved that things didn't work out between you two."

Me: "What? Come on, that's so not cool. He's a nice guy. He treated me well and everything. Hey, are we gonna make it in time for our dinner reservation, or what? If we miss it, it's Ryan's fault *again*...."

Melody: "Seriously, you'd think he's a girl or something, the way he's always so late."

Ryan: "I said I was sorry, guys. I was in the middle of a really intense game of Warcraft online, and I didn't realize what time it was."

Bryan: "Yeah, well, at least he remembered there was a specific time we were leaving. Desi here forgot to tell me what the plan was.... Can everyone just tell *me* from now on?"

Me: "I feel for you, Bryan. We shared a room for so many years so I know just how she is."

Desi: "I know, I know. I don't *mean* to forget things. But I shared a room with *you too*, and at least I'm not known as Captain Minutes."

Laughter all around at my expense. She was right, though. I can be a nut about keeping to a set schedule. I guess I deserve the title sometimes.

Gregory: "Yeah, the good captain can get pretty intense sometimes, but at least she can make decisions when she needs to...MELODY!"

Melody: "Yeah, yeah...I know. Not my strong point. But I usually do end up making a good decision—it just takes me a little while."

Ryan: "A little while? Uh, right. Deon could date and dump Chuck three more times before you'd even be able to decide on what guy you'd like to go out with."

Just then a cell phone rang, and I think we were all a bit grateful for it. I overheard my brother-in-law on his cell phone amid the chatter. "I don't know, I'll ask her." Bryan hung up the phone. Very nonchalantly he turned to me and said, "I have a buddy in town visiting his aunt, my mom's best friend. We grew up together, and he's a really cool guy. Would you want to meet him?"

This caught me off-guard. "Where's he from?"

"Alaska," came the casual answer.

"What would I have in common with a guy from *Alaska*?" I asked.

My dad glanced back at me from the driver's seat and said very seriously, "Deon, you never know. It's best to just meet people and then make your decision."

"All right, all right.... Can we meet him first, *before* we agree to let him hang out with us the rest of the night? I don't want to be stuck with him all night if it's clearly not happening." I wasn't going to be caught in an awkward scenario at the stroke of midnight, if I could help it.

"Do you think we'll get along? I mean, what's he like?" I wondered out loud.

"I know you'll like him, unless he's a dork for five minutes or something," Bryan said, chuckling.

If my skeptical brother-in-law was vouching for him, he must be pretty decent. Bryan wasn't going to let just *anyone* into this family, and neither were any of the others for that matter. With any tight family comes the inevitable rapid gunfire of opinions, regardless of whether you want them. After everyone had a say, I decided I was willing to take the risk. I wasn't even sure if I was ready to start dating again, much less meet some crazy Alaskan—for all intents and purposes I'm a city girl through and through. I couldn't see this going anywhere. I had nothing to lose, though. No expectations, no disappointments. And if I didn't like him, I wasn't likely to ever run into him again. That was a plus. I couldn't see any harm in just *casually* stopping by, as long as there was the strict understanding that I could bolt in a moment's notice if necessary. No pressure, I was promised.

There's nothing like eight people walking through a door complete with crazy New Year's Eve party hats and blowers and all to really downplay a situation. What an entrance. I wasn't exactly sure how to feel about all this, and yet here I was. I had to at least be cordial. After the initial hellos to Bryan's family for the sake of "playing it cool," I decided it was now acceptable to glance over to the stranger sitting across the room on the fireplace ledge. (I'd secretly spotted him the second I walked through the door.) Timing is everything. Our eyes met, and all six foot four inches of him stood to shake my hand and introduce himself.

"I'm Kevin."

We moved into substantial conversation quickly and painlessly. This was oddly like talking with someone I'd grown up with. Before long, Kevin had invited me up to Alaska after my final semester of school when I graduated with my master's, and I was comfortable enough to accept. Totally unlike me. Strange how this was happening so quickly, and we'd only just met. And did I mention that he was hot, and planning to transfer to the university in Utah? Stranger things have happened, I wondered.

Many hours later, and with a distinct passing of one year to the next, as the party horns and background chatter faded, two simple people sat alone in deep conversation. No twenty-questions, no chitchat. There's so much that just doesn't need to be said. So much that's just somehow understood. No games. No muddled emotions. No clutter to get in the way. Just two people who are oddly compatible and have somehow stumbled across each other.

A couple of priceless days later, I was on my way back to New York for school, shocked and amazed, but mostly grateful for the funny way things turn out sometimes. Five months and thousands of cell phone minutes later, we knew we were meant for each other. Everything seemed to be falling into place. Kevin was preparing to transfer down to Utah, and no sooner than the ink could dry on my diploma, I was going to be on my way to Alaska to meet his family.

First things first, focus on graduating. My most overwhelming requirement to graduate was left to the end—a final seventy-five-minute recital with my sister Desirae. The two years required for our master's degrees were dedicated to learning and performing music written for two pianists. Desi and I had always felt this was our niche and were thrilled when Juilliard allowed us to focus our efforts here. This was unprecedented, we were told. We purposefully set our joint recital as close to graduation as we could so that my parents could fly in from Utah to attend both monumental occasions. Months and months were invested into preparing, and knowing that all our closest friends and family would be in attendance made it all the more rewarding. Well, almost all of those closest to us. All except for one.

The day for our recital couldn't come soon enough. As far as I was concerned, it was the final hurdle I had to overcome in order to begin the next chapter in my life. It would simply be a matter of pushing through, and before I'd know it, it would all be over. Well, that's what I kept telling myself to ease the pressure, but it wasn't exactly helping. I can't remember ever being so nervous and excited at the same time—excited because I was almost past the pressures and requirements of Juilliard, and nervous because of the impending doom of having to perform this music in front of real people. But in just a few more days, I would be off to Alaska for a couple of weeks, my six years at Juilliard far behind me. It was all so close I could taste it.

Desi and I practiced all we could, sensing the end so closely in sight. Before we knew it the day was upon us. The dreaded yet anticipated day. In the early afternoon we dropped by to see my parents at their hotel for moral support, but besides that brief distraction we were solely focused on the task at hand—graduating.

We had to throw some of the music together quicker than proved comfortable, and so felt less confident than we would have wanted. *Oh, well.* We already had one foot out the door anyway. As we came to the final few minutes of the recital, I could sense my mind literally beginning to shut down into "hibernate-mode." I just needed to hang on a tiny bit longer....

Finally the applause came from our slightly biased family and friends. The stress was officially over, and I was free—free from exams and teachers and boring required classes. Free from the confines of our one-building campus and tiny practice rooms. *Elation* can't describe the intense feelings at seeing my six-year Juilliard project successfully come to a close. I had invested so much of myself through countless hours of hard work, all the while subjecting my emotions to a series of frightening roller-coaster rides. I had lived through my share of disappointments and shed too many tears to count. I had come to New York City a naïve seventeen-year-old from a small town in Utah with no clue as to who I was, as a person or musician. I was leaving here a reliable, self-sufficient adult, confident in her abilities as an artist. I had literally grown up within these walls. I'd learned a lot, and was taking far more with me than I'd come with. I'd served my time well.

Desi and I took a celebratory bow and headed offstage. It was over. Almost as quickly as we were out of view, the audience urged us to return for another bow. I looked out and was humbled by the smiling faces of so many who cared about us; people who had been there with us through it all. I felt lucky to have such amazing support. Bryan emerged from the audience carrying a beautiful bouquet of flowers—*Aww, how thoughtful. Desi will love that.* But behind him in the shadows was another.

I strained to see anything other than basic shapes in the dim light. Slowly a face began to emerge from the darkness. My heart nearly stopped beating. *It couldn't be—it just couldn't.* Carrying an equally impressive bouquet and an even bigger smile was Kevin, my Alaskan. As he reached the stage and joined me, I was overwhelmed and speechless. This must be some sort of wonderful dream where both of my worlds collide.

The crowd was still cheering, none the wiser of the magnitude of the situation and the person before them. Stunned and amazed, I began to walk off the stage again. Taking my first steps in that direction, I felt a slight tug and heard a faint "you're not going anywhere." Before I realized what was happening, Kevin was on one knee in front of everyone and reaching for my left hand. My beautiful flowers dropped to the stage as the crowd began to cheer even louder. My heart jumped as he began, "Deondra, I'll love you forever. I'd be honored if you'd be my wife. Will you marry me?"

"YES!" I all but yelled as I jumped into his arms, the crowd cheering its loudest yet. He slipped the beautiful diamond ring onto my shaky finger. The ring, like Kevin, was perfect for me.

Beaming from ear to ear, I felt as if we were in a completely different world consisting of just the two of us. It must have been mere seconds, but so much was said as we looked into each other's eyes. Our lives had just officially begun, together.

Encore, encore!

Caught up in my emotions, I had forgotten all about the witnesses to our private moment. With a quick nod to Desi, we agreed to comply with the audience's gracious request. I sheepishly and begrudgingly handed my beautiful ring back to Kevin for a few brief moments. How on earth was I going to focus on playing a piece after all this? He chuckled at the funny gesture of receiving the ring he had just given me, and I made my way back to the piano. This was to be the most emotional encore of my life. I was sure of it. I was playing it *just* for him.

In less than twenty-four hours, it seemed the whole school knew of the happenings of one insignificant recital. With a student body of less than 800, word travels fast.

Something this out of the ordinary was bound to create some buzz. We will forever be immortalized within the walls of Juilliard. I had definitely left my mark. Quite an exit, if I do say so myself.

As I stood in my graduation gown the following day, I couldn't help but look down at the ring that will forever grace my finger. I could only imagine what our life together would have in store. If you can tell anything from our beginnings, it's destined to be quite a tale—eventful, unpredictable, and *never* dull: a most unconventional path.

※　※　※

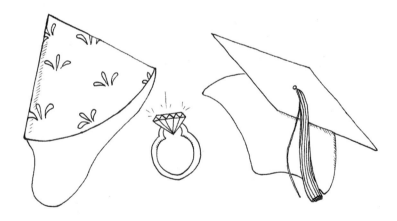

My brother Gregory and I were very close growing up. When it came time for him to go off to college, I was encouraged to audition for the Juilliard School at the same time. I was fifteen at my entrance audition, and sixteen when I was accepted into the college that fall with my brother. My young age caused problems for Juilliard's administration. After the acceptance of a fifteen-year-old the previous year who had failed every class, the school would not permit another to be accepted without a new set of rules.

Names have been changed to protect the innocent.

L.S.D.

BY MELODY BROWN

New York City
2000–2002

Let's just say that before I went to college, I was sort of sheltered. An international piano competition in Champaign, Illinois, was one of my first trips out of Utah. I was the girl who thought the glass of lemonade at the winner's reception tasted funny because it was carbonated. I'd always hated carbonation. Little did I realize at the time that this would go down as my first sip of champagne. I vowed it to be my last; the taste haunts me to this day.

Let's fast-forward a few years....

"Please, please! Will you stash this? They're coming in, like, five minutes. The R.A.s never check *your* room."

The look in their eyes as they held that bottle of alcohol was sheer panic. If they were caught, they'd be kicked out of the L.S.D.

The Lithuanian School of Dance—L.S.D.—is the most prestigious dance school in the country. Made up of ballerinas thirteen to eighteen years old whose parents sent them to New York City to train with the best, it is a school of discipline and intense instruction. It was here where I stood eyeing the bottle of alcohol in my fifteen-year-old neighbor's hand. It was also here where I thought, "How in the world did she even get alcohol?"

You're probably wondering why I, a pianist, was living in a school of dance. According to Juilliard, having an underage student was like having a juvenile delinquent. My preferential treatment for coming into the college at sixteen was living with the L.S.D. students. At first it did seem like preferential treatment, with the enticingly bigger room, more food money, and quieter floor. Little did I know that I was under twenty-four-hour surveillance.

Housed in the same dormitory building as the Juilliard School—where I had just been accepted as a freshman in piano—the Lithuanian School of Dance provided "adequate supervision." According to Juilliard, it didn't matter what my background was, how trustworthy I could be, how much my parents could vouch for my responsibility, or even if I was Amish. Juilliard was not liable for me, and I needed supervision. "Adequate" consisted of video cameras, a separate security desk and check-in for entering and leaving the building, flipped color-coordinated cards for when I was "in" or "out," locked elevator floors, nightly room-checks, and yes, a 10 p.m. curfew. I was making strides in my life: my first year of college and my first curfew. You can imagine my joy. I was coming from a home where I was completely trusted by my parents, constantly told by my mom that I was an "old soul," and deemed one of the most responsible members in the family...to *this*? We had no choice. My parents relinquished the keys of a lifetime of guidance and sound judgment into the hands of a school.

I cried to them that first night on the designated pay phone. Luckily I had a quarter.

"Ten o'clock is when Juilliard students are just getting started!" was what I blurted out in a hurry. I didn't know how long my extra dimes would last on the phone.

It was true. The movies, mafia games, late-night food runs, and endless "do you think he likes me" conversations with new friends hadn't even begun to take place before I was banished to my room, "or else." Being scared, I took "or else" seriously. All I could imagine was house arrest and chains. I never wanted to find out what the real consequences would be, so I complied. My Juilliard friends kept wondering where I would vanish to so early in the evening. Only too many times I would try to say quietly,

"I have curfew."

"What?"

After a few more rounds of this, *everyone* could hear over the loud music or conversation, "I HAVE CURFEW!"

"*In college?*" Instantaneous laughter.

Let's go back to where we started. When my suitemates held that precious bottle of alcohol in front of me, I had a choice. They were right; the R.A.s (Resident Advisors) never did check my room. I had been established as the "good Mormon girl." Never having missed curfew and always trying to obey the rules actually gave me a few special privileges, one of which being that my room was always deemed "clean." I had learned early on in my family's household that the reward for good behavior was usually more freedom. I was pleased to see that it was working here as well.

I realize that we're all taught to refuse drugs or alcohol when we're underage. But in my mind it was always maimed, goth-looking people in dark rooms blaring Marilyn Manson who did the offering. Here I had two beautiful, desperate girls standing at my door, handing me a bottle of alcohol. My preconceived black-and-white answer wasn't so black and white anymore.

"After all, *I* won't be drinking it," was what I kept thinking. The bottle was stashed under a pile of clothes in my closet. I did feel a tinge of guilt for abusing my hard-earned freedom, but yeah, I stashed it anyway. When I accepted, I didn't fully realize that house arrest would be out of the question if I were caught. A cardboard box on the street was more the reality. Still, I hid that bottle because my two neighbors and I knew what my real choice was: I could be the "cool" good girl or the "goody two-shoes" girl who would forever be blamed for getting two dancers kicked out of L.S.D. Funny enough, it never did cross my mind that I could get kicked out instead.

When the R.A. had left and my suitemate recovered her most valued possession, I was trusted implicitly. After this single stash, I was on speaking terms with a girl who had never uttered a word to me before. How simple it was to gain "friends."

After a while I grew used to the happenings of L.S.D. When Thanksgiving break rolled around, I wasn't surprised to hear what took place in my room while I was gone. Of course, this was still early on in my L.S.D. experience; Anna was my roommate then.

Anna was pretty nice; at least we got along well. When I first set foot on the L.S.D. floors, my guide divulged that they had put us together because we were both "prodigies." I never considered myself such, but the word in regard to her made me think she was pretty incredible. I was told that at fifteen she was already apprenticing with the very elite New York City Ballet, a rare achievement. I later lost her as a roommate when she was fully accepted into the company at sixteen, something almost unheard of.

"Because she's so gifted, we thought you two would get along. It's hard for some girls here to accept a roommate who is so far beyond them already."

Warning flags went up immediately. The flags waved as we spent an entire evening admiring her dancing on

VHS tapes shortly after we'd met. Full of never-ending conversation, she would tell me about how people at home never understood her, and why she *had* to be at L.S.D.

"They just don't understand that I exceeded my training back home. I mean, I'm even at the top here!"

I was starting to see why they had put us together. This girl was really good, and she knew it. I could see it on tape as she pointed out the highlights. I guess the L.S.D. figured I could compete with that. However, I wasn't about to get into the New York City Ballet. I had just been accepted to Juilliard. In my mind plenty of kids did this every year. She, on the other hand, was the best in her school and receiving flak from the other girls because of it.

Anna and I did get along, even though she and her friends considered me as the "new girl." Being such, I wasn't in their circle of trust, so they kept their distance. As a result they chose to smoke pot in the room when I was out of town. I appreciated this and the fact that they opened the windows while they did it. There's nothing like smelling pot in your sheets.

Over Thanksgiving break I have to say I was relieved to be gone. The R.A. smelled the pot and caught my roommate and a few other girls smoking. The geniuses closed the window because they were cold. Anna divulged the whole story when I came back. I was surprised she was even around to tell it.

"Can you believe it? 'If you promise not to do it again' was all we got. We didn't even have to call our parents!"

The new, sweet R.A. was responsible for this slight warning. There was only one thing worse than getting caught, and that was calling your parents to clue them in on the news. The girls thought they could take advantage of the new "let's be friends" R.A. Luckily Anna was out of town a few weeks later when this same R.A. caught these girls again. Only this time, it wasn't pot. These fifteen-year-old girls were caught with coke. I started second-guessing whether "coke" actually meant cocaine. It seemed much more likely that these girls would get their hands on bottles of Coke, rather than their noses on actual cocaine. But then, a bottle of Coke doesn't get you kicked out of L.S.D. I started to feel bad for their parents. Here they spent thousands of dollars a year for a potential ballet superstar, only to have paid for a possible lifetime of drug habits.

After the expelled had left, their news following them, I realized I had problems of my own. Anna had started getting serious with her boyfriend, Matthias. I failed to mention that there are the token boys in L.S.D. There are those who are man enough to choose dance as their profession, and those who love the men in their profession. Anna found the former. I tried to relay to her that I was fine with them becoming "more serious" when she started hinting at needing the room to herself and, well, Matthias. After all, in my head I was in college now, even though by this point we were both only sixteen. She did try hard to be as inconspicuous as she could. Whenever I found myself in the room with them, she would quickly find reasons to leave. Going to Matthias's room to work on difficult moves from class was always a good reason. I had the sense that they were indeed working on moves; it's just questionable whether they were the ones from class.

Only once did I come back to my room and find the door locked. I saw a mirage of red flags covering *that* door. We usually kept it unlocked, since the most valuable thing was probably my "princess bedding." I became nervous when I went from the door handle to the keys in my pocket. I tried to fidget with the handle as long as possible to give adequate time and warning to those inside. When I finally did open the door, I found poor Anna and Matthias struggling to put the bare necessities on. I was mad at myself for ill timing at the handle. Apologizing profusely for interrupting their rehearsal, I grabbed the music I needed and bee-lined for the door.

Shortly after this, I lost Anna as a roommate. So did Matthias. She went on to bigger and better things after she was accepted into the New York City Ballet. As she told it, "I'm out of here. I'm moving into a studio apartment next week." It made sense to our sixteen-year-old minds. She did have a salary now. She could do whatever she wanted. I was in awe that her dance took her from a trailer back home, to a full scholarship at the L.S.D., to a studio apartment in New York City. If only all of us in the arts could be so lucky. If only I could be so lucky. She was shaking off the L.S.D. right as most were just coming in. She didn't have to play by the rules anymore. She was free of all authority as a young teenager. I envied her.

While moving out she was downstairs saying some of her goodbyes. I was waiting for the elevator farther away, privy to her conversation but not wanting to interrupt. These girls, like most in the L.S.D., didn't realize I was her roommate. Actually, most didn't even realize I was on their floor. Juilliard and L.S.D. were confused as to who I was. In an attempt to attach myself to Juilliard, I chose not to associate much with the L.S.D. I didn't know these particular girls, so they probably didn't know me. They did seem genuinely excited for Anna, though. The conversation ended with "we're so happy for you!" as they hurried in the elevator with me. The doors closed, and all of a sudden Anna was equivalent to gum stuck to their *pointe* shoes.

"Can you believe that *she* got into the city ballet?"

"*No*. She's not even all that great. She thinks she is, though."

"She's also not all that thin. She'll have a rude awakening there."

The girl with the last comment had a point. One thing I did learn from Anna was that unlike the other girls in L.S.D., who fainted in the cafeteria under the weight of their food trays, she prided herself in being strong, not waif-thin. The night we admired her dancing on VHS was the night we talked about starving and barfing, the eating disorders that ruled L.S.D. It's a dance epidemic. The once-a-month cafeteria-collapsings were a testament to its existence. At the time I never understood how a few leaves of lettuce could warrant fainting. Then again, I did start to see a lot more styrofoam dishes being used on those trays. Anna could handle the weight of her real dishes, and the food on them, because she knew she was stronger and better than the rest. Her cafeteria tray was never as sparse as others, since eating healthily was a source of pride.

When Anna moved out I never really saw her again. I would briefly catch fellow L.S.D. residents talking about her in the latest ballet, but the elevator wasn't long enough to eavesdrop successfully. I did hear, however, in my sophomore year at Juilliard that a critic for *The New York Times* had reviewed the New York City Ballet. Some idiot wrote that the whole company needed to lose weight. Is it right to suppose that a fat old man sitting at his computer has that much clout? I briefly saw Anna after that. Her eyes had lost their brightness and looked sunken, her arms and legs tired and malnourished. The only thing I could think was "Oh, Anna, you succumbed." A critic drove a girl to starve herself, keeping alive the notion that all true dancers have to be rail-thin. It hurts to imagine her alone in the studio apartment, hearing the words of that critic over and over again in her mind. There was no one there to reassure her that she didn't need to take part. No one to love her and tell her that so much of her talent was due to her health and lust for life.

Didn't the critics know that eating was already a prominent theme in the life of a dancer? It's all I ever heard at the L.S.D. "Did you see what was on her tray?" was a regular elevator topic. "I heard she's not eating" was another popular one. If it wasn't how much you were eating, it was how little. I was annoyed when I couldn't use either of our two bathrooms because one suitemate was taking a shower, and the other was barfing.

I was also haunted and annoyed when I couldn't open my window all the way. Thick plastic cording screwed into the window prevented this. It would only crack open about two inches, whereas before it would crack open to about four. I and everyone else would forever remember the girl who *tried* to commit suicide for this. Evidently she could fit her whole body out the window. Her head stopped her from going through with it, since it couldn't make it past the four inches. They found her like that. All of us had to live with her demented memory whenever we cracked our windows open for some air. If it hadn't already been tried, I think a lot more students would've been found squishing themselves through even the two inches. It was like this place had a permanent rain cloud over it. Or rather, everyone was walking around with individual rain clouds. I could feel my own forming. I ran into many girls crying. At night I would get so down at my situation that I couldn't help but cry too. The only ray of sunlight at the L.S.D. was a cute little pepper plant. Too bad someone came and stole it. I'd rather someone stole my "princess bedding" than my cute, happy pepper plant. We were all clawing for happiness. Everything from drugs to a cheerful plant was fair game.

Along with the theft, gossip ran rampant at the L.S.D. I knew it firsthand when Jane, one of my suitemates, provided months of material for discussion. It all started when she sneaked out on a Friday night. This was the series of events her ingenious escape comprised:

First, you must know that a person COULD NOT get off of the L.S.D. floors once they were locked. The buttons were dead. You could stand there for hours waiting; it didn't help your situation. One *could* get *onto* the floors, however. Once in the elevator, you could press the fourteenth floor, L.S.D.'s entrance, and those doors would open at all times day and night. Thus the person standing on fourteen aimlessly pushing dead buttons could have the elevator magically open, if someone inside happened to press that floor.

Jane had a drama student from Juilliard press the fourteenth floor from inside the elevator. (Sadly, I had introduced her to this guy, who had a perverse obsession with

L.S.D. girls.) She made a sprint for the doors, as Kristoff, the
drama student, relentlessly pressed "close door" before the
L.S.D. security guard could catch her.

She didn't come back that night or the next. I
wondered if she'd finally escaped our prison. I started to
revere her as our Joan of Arc. There was a strong urge to rally
troops of girls around her armed with tutu flags.

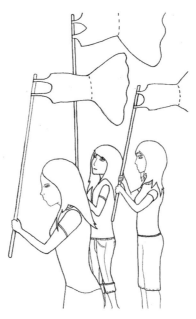

All reveries were shattered when my heroine returned
to L.S.D. I never knew her punishment; I figured it was
another version of house arrest. She was just relieved it didn't
come down to calling her parents. All in all we thought she'd
gotten off pretty easily.

No one, not even Jane, could've hidden the *real*
consequence of her escapades. The call to her parents did
eventually come. So did the news that she was leaving L.S.D.

Within six months she would have a baby in her arms,
an individual who would forever represent freedom and
dashed dreams all in one. Hearing her cry through the wall

for days haunted me. Without desiring to, I also heard many phone conversations with her mom; that's if one can call yelling and crying "conversation." With no phones in the rooms, and few girls owning cell phones at that time, she spent her afternoons huddled over the community phone on the floor of our suite. With her back propped up against the fridge, she spent days reliving her mistake. The fridge might've blocked the torment in her face, but I'll never forget the agony in her voice.

The same girl who once held the bottle of alcohol at my door was now a few feet away from me, broken. I thought I'd helped save Jane that night. Now, glancing in her direction, I knew I'd only saved face.

Pieces of Jane were scattered in tears all over the floor. I was beginning to see cracks in *my* once-happy exterior. The bars on our doors made us all so desperate for love, for happiness. We were sent for priceless training only to start losing ourselves in the process. My black-and-white world was suddenly so gray. I didn't know what I believed anymore, whom to trust, and where inspiration could be found. Piano playing began to consume me, since all I had to replace it with was teen pregnancy, eating disorders, drug addiction, and depression. Music was everything, and it wasn't going well. I couldn't play anymore when I didn't know what to live for. Suddenly everything I had grown up to have faith in crumbled around me. I kept trying to live the way I had been raised, but I felt like a hypocrite since the root of it all was shriveling. Why was I still trying to be good? What was the point of morality, of virtue?

These were some of the darkest years of my life. I felt crippled, trapped, and depressed. It felt as though I would always be stuck at the L.S.D. At one point it was so bad that not a day went by when I didn't break down emotionally.

My parents could only know from a distance what was going on. One night I called saying I didn't want to be there anymore. I wasn't happy, I wasn't good enough, and on top of it all, I was trapped. I'll forever remember what my mom told me that night.

"Melody, it's gotten to a point where no one can help you anymore; not your teachers, friends, family, or now even yourself. I think you need to let go of it all and remember where your talents have always come from."

For the first time in what felt like years, I prayed. In the midst of Jane, in the midst of Anna, in the midst of so many problems, I tried to get outside of myself, to remember what I once knew. That night I knelt by my bed with the glow of Christmas lights sparkling through my tears. The small lights shining through the blackness of the room put my seemingly dark life in perspective. The warmth I felt when I opened a dusty forgotten book is forever ingrained in my mind. The words I just happened to start reading were so specifically for me:

Wait patiently on the Lord, for your prayers have entered into the ears of the Lord. Therefore, He giveth this promise unto you, with an immutable covenant that [your prayers] shall be fulfilled; and all things wherewith you have been afflicted shall work together for your good, and to my name's glory, saith the Lord.

I wasn't alone. I knew it.

The tears Jane shed by the fridge, or Lydia by the window before attempting suicide, or Anna by her mirror, are all memorials walked over and long forgotten. In my mind they live on as stains of loneliness. Yet there is one place that illuminates the memory of those floors, one place where tears were knelt over and conquered. Here was where everything seemed worth it in the end. For I realized one thing that I would forever grasp onto. I wasn't alone. I'll never be alone.

*   *   *

*Without paying a cent of tuition, he would come to my classes
with me in the afternoons and sit through required concerts. He'd raise
his hand and answer questions, or even ask for clarification when the
teacher was confusing, and no one ever gave it a second thought. As far
as the student body and faculty were concerned, Cory Rivard was a
fulltime student at the Juilliard School.*

CORY RIVARD

BY GREGORY BROWN

Suite 1801
The Juilliard Dorms
New York City
2000–2001

New York can be a bewildering place for a kid in his
late teens, but the oddities of the city pale in comparison to
the more terrifying world of perplexities that occupy the heart
during those difficult years of youth and transition.

As I started my first few semesters of school in the
big city, I was on my own and living by my own rules for the
first time in my life. Even though I had three siblings going
to Juilliard with me at the time, I was still by myself to figure
out what was best for me. Initially, this was an exciting
thought, being a sheltered kid from Utah and never having
experienced such freedom before. I could wake up when I
wanted to, I could eat what I wanted to, I could hang out with
whomever I wanted, and in a city where it's easy to fall
through the cracks, I could essentially do whatever I wanted.

With freedom and change came questions. I started
questioning almost everything I knew, or thought I knew,
about who I was, and when it really came down to it, I saw
that I didn't understand myself at all. It was as though I had

fallen off a boat into the middle of a vast ocean, disoriented and unsure of which direction to swim.

I first tried swimming in the direction of the "cool kids"—maybe being one of them would help me see who I was—but while their welcome was warm, it didn't take long before I saw that I was little more than a faceless accomplice to folly in their eyes. Next, I changed course and swam in the general direction of a girlfriend, but how can you possibly understand someone else in a relationship when you don't even understand what makes *you* tick? Now, you might ask, "Why not just swim back to the comfort of the boat you came from?" That would seem like the logical solution, wouldn't it? Well, I eventually came to it on my own, but it took a few kicks in the butt to get there.

One of the first of these swift kicks to the butt came running through the door of my dorm-room suite as I watched TV one night during the first part of freshman year. This kid seemed strangely familiar to me, though I wouldn't understand why until years later. His name was Cory Rivard. He was from Canada but was in town visiting a classmate of mine. I believe the first thing he yelled as he entered my suite common room was some lame comment about a couple in the building across the way that had left their curtains open. He went running from suite to suite through the dorms like a mentally challenged Paul Revere, "warning" everyone about the sideshow across the street just in case they were interested. Yeah, it was immature, but his enthusiasm in itself was pretty funny and even covetable in a way.

In the days that followed, I saw him around quite a bit, and we got to be pretty good friends. As time passed, he started hanging out with me just as often as he hung out with the friend he had come to visit. He was probably the most confident and outgoing person I had ever met in my life, and as these were qualities that I conspicuously lacked, I kind of hoped I might soak up a bit of it and learn a thing or two.

As it turned out, Cory had only bought a one-way bus ticket to New York and had no immediate obligations back in Canada, so he was going to stay as long as he possibly could. He had very little money and no way of making more, but he was much more clever than the people who make the rules. New York is not a cheap place to live by any stretch of the imagination, but he managed to survive in one of the most expensive parts of the city for two-thirds of my freshman year on nothing more than a couple of hundred dollars and a lot of smooth talking. He started out by sleeping on the couch of his Canadian friend, Mike, but Mike's other roomies didn't take too well to having a semi-permanent ninth suitemate. My suite—1801—was a much different story, however.

That year suite 1801 was without a doubt the most infamous suite the Juilliard dorm building had seen in a lot of years. It was the only suite in the building that every student knew by name, and at any given time, day or night, you could probably count twice the amount of the people who actually lived there—oftentimes many more. The R.A. was criminally lenient, and the actual residents of 1801 were as infamous as the suite itself. The combination of these two factors, plus one other key element—a Sony PlayStation—made my suite the most communal area in the dorms.

The place was an utter trash heap. No one ever cleaned, because 1) we were just too lazy; 2) after a certain point, you don't even know how to go about making a dent in the filth; and 3) half of the mess wasn't even made by 1801 residents. I'm honestly surprised that everyone who lived there didn't come down with hepatitis or something, because there was trash everywhere—moldy food strewn across the floor, half-empty bottles of booze lying all over (and half the kids who hung out there were underage), and don't even get me started with the bathrooms. You'd probably be safer doing your business in a chemical waste plant than you would be in 1801.

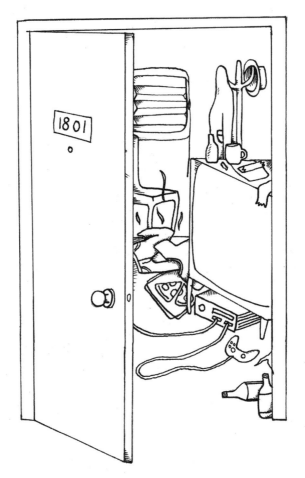

Still, once Mike's roommates forced Cory to leave, the first place he came was 1801. He was there for most of each day already, so everyone who spent time there already liked him. Plus, considering the filth, no one would likely even notice some random guy sleeping on the couch. He stayed on that couch for months, and the only people who cared were the security guards at the entrance of the dorms.

It was dorm policy that guests can't stay longer than one week, so once the guards started noticing that the same kid without proper school I.D. kept squeezing through the entrance gate every day, they began to get on his case. He was able to sweet-talk the female guards for a while, but once weeks turned into months, it became an all-out battle between Cory and the dorm guards.

If his free lodging was impressive in itself, his methods of attaining food were legendary. I don't know that he paid a dime for food during the entire time he was in New York. He knew that the ballet students who shared the dorm building with Juilliard had much bigger meal plans than the Juilliard kids. This was ridiculous, because those girls hardly ate a thing, so the money was basically going to waste. Cory exploited this tragedy to the fullest. He would stand in the cafeteria during meal times and wait for some unsuspecting ballet dancer to walk in. Once deciding on a target, it was time to turn on the old Canadian charm. After the girl predictably grabbed her small salad and a bottle of water, he'd find a flirtatious yet non-threatening way of asking her if he could use the rest of her allotted meal money to grab a bit of food. The plan was utterly genius, and it worked almost every time.

There was hardly a student in the whole school who wasn't absolutely convinced that Cory studied at Juilliard. It wasn't only the students that he managed to convince, either; he had many of the teachers going too. Without paying a cent of tuition, he would come to my classes with me in the afternoons and sit through required concerts. He'd raise his hand to answer questions, or even ask for clarification when the teacher was confusing, and no one ever gave it a second thought. As far as the student body and faculty were concerned, Cory Rivard was a fulltime student at the Juilliard School.

Every time we hung out was like its own little adventure, as he could always find a way to have insane amounts of fun without spending any money whatsoever. Between pulling video game all-nighters, exploring Times

Square at four in the morning (which I don't suggest; I've never been that scared in my life), sneaking past security guards, and tipping hotel bellboys to help us play pranks on sleeping friends, the two of us had the most epic adventures imaginable, but we both knew it couldn't last forever. Sooner or later, Cory would have to go back to Canada, because no matter how many people he had convinced, he still wasn't a Juilliard student, and the game would eventually have to come to an end. Plus he was almost out of money and only had just enough for the bus ticket back.

While Cory Rivard definitely had his immature side, he was really just a genuinely nice kid with a huge heart. Before he came to New York, I had spent so much time trying to be friends with superficial, fake people, that by the time he showed up, I was more than ready for someone real—someone I could trust who actually cared about me as a friend. I already had what I was looking for in that respect when it came to my family, but for some reason I just wouldn't allow myself to be satisfied with that as I struggled in the vast ocean for something else to grab hold of.

As I said, there was something familiar about Cory when I first met him, and it wasn't until long after he left that I realized just what it was. He was me—a kid searching for something, lost in a world he didn't understand, trying to figure out who he was and where he belonged. He had fallen in love with the very life I complained so much about and wanted to escape—my school, my family, my music—and I could tell that those things were not going to be waiting for him back in Canada. He was trying to escape his life, and I was trying to escape aspects of mine. We crossed paths, and for a few months we were able to inspire each other in our own small ways.

Cory helped open my eyes to what I truly had. Yes, I was an awkward kid; yes, I was struggling mightily with my music at the time and was second-guessing why I was at Juilliard in the first place; and yes, I still didn't understand who I was or what my full potential held, but look at what I *did* have. People who cared about me. A really great school to educate me. A talent that could uplift and bring light to sad and tired eyes. At the time, I was a blank slate capable of becoming so much more than I was allowing myself to be. He showed me that with a little confidence and some faith in my capacity, I could really do almost anything. I know that sounds cliché, but hey, if he can live in Manhattan for months on end for free, then heck, maybe anything really *is* possible.

On the morning he left, I awoke to the sound of "New York, New York" by Frank Sinatra coming from the suite common room. This was nothing new, as the first thing he did every morning was blast that song, but this time it was a little different. He wasn't singing at the top of his lungs, and he wasn't banging on my door to wake me up. I hopped out of bed and stepped out of my room. There was Cory, stuffing a bunch of dingy clothes into a torn duffel bag. It was probably the first time I had seen him without a smile on his face. Realizing how hard it must be for him to leave New York, I took the opportunity to assume his role for few moments, belting out, "If I can make it there, I'll make it anywhere" at the top of my lungs, and he instantly snapped out of it. Side by side, each with an arm across the other's shoulder, we stepped onto the couch cushions, faced the window overlooking the Hudson River, and hollered the rest of the song as loud as we could.

We knew we'd both be just fine. He and I had no idea in what separate directions our young lives would lead us, but somehow it felt like anything was possible all the same. Suddenly, my newfound freedom didn't seem quite so scary, and I knew which direction I needed to be swimming. I belonged with family, I belonged with friends who cared about me, I belonged with music, and I belonged with the values that were a part of me. I also knew that once Cory and I finally gave up attempting to escape our lives by trading places and trying to be what we weren't, we would begin to see the extent of our own potentials and the beauty of our individual capacities.

Five years later, Cory made his fourth trip to New York City to attend the master's graduation of the friends he had grown so close to back in freshman year. Everyone still knew who he was, and each time he came to visit, it was like he had never left. In a final act of rebellion on my last day as a Juilliard student, Cory and I planned one ultimate farewell prank.

As the class of 2006 lined up on the steps of the school to take the group photo that would be enshrined in the hallways of Juilliard for years to come, I couldn't help but smirk a little. If you ever happen to find yourself wandering past the registrar's office at Juilliard, be sure to stop and pick out the photo of the '06 class. Right in the center near the back, you'll find a random guy who, for some reason, is the only person not wearing a cap and gown. Hmm…. I wonder who that could be.

*   *   *

*The bond between two sisters can be stronger than just about
anything. This connection is somehow ingrained in our souls and can
surface at any moment to offer shelter. It supersedes all personal wants
and desires, and has a way of making even the most tragic situations less
severe. Sisters understand each other in a way few others can. They will
give up anything if necessary to protect their other half.*

SUPERHERO
BY DEONDRA BROWN

Houston, Texas
Spring 1987

"It's almost time," Desi whispered as we sneaked as
quietly as we could past Mom's slightly cracked bedroom
door. We were supposed to be taking our afternoon nap, as
Mom was taking her much-needed one at the same time.
(Five kids under the age of six must be draining even for a
mother as well-equipped to deal with them as she.) But we
had something other than a nap on our minds, as we did every
day at this time.

We crossed the living room, careful to avoid each
creak in the hardwood floors. We had come to know every
one of them well. You couldn't be too careful—Mom was a
light sleeper, so we tried extra hard not to tip her off to our
escapades. She had superhuman hearing, we were sure. We
crouched and sat on the floor, beginning our daily "nap" as
we always did. We knew our jobs only too well.

Desi flipped on the power button, and I quickly
lowered the volume. We had it down to a science, never
letting the sound escape far enough into the silence for
anyone to hear. The anticipation was likely to kill us. We
flipped the channel just in time to see the opening credits. We
never wanted to miss even a second.

And there she was in all her glory. We jumped to our feet, anxious and ready to assist her in every way. We knew her moves in precise detail. With every jump and spin, we were right there beside her. We blocked every bullet using our bulletproof wrist guards too, just like her. She pummeled every guy with the help of her two little skinny blonde sidekicks. We were a team.

Wonder Woman—the perfect blend of strength and true humanity. And she was a *girl*. No one would dare mess with her, but she could show compassion to even the worst of criminals. She was indestructible.

In thirty minutes, the world would go from devastating to as it should be, with the assistance of our well-hidden nap-dodging. The regular world needed her, and so did ours. She represented all that was right with them both. She was our little secret, and outside of our daily "nap" we spoke of her only in whispers. We religiously practiced our moves in our free time as we played, just in case she needed us. We would be ready at a moment's notice.

We collected our money in earnest that night, counting each coin carefully by the small amount of light cascading from our closet. We had just enough. Mom was making an important trip to the fabric store the next day, and we were going to be ready.

We picked out just the right one, and oh, was it pretty! It was a beautiful mixture of our two favorite colors— turquoise and purple. We were both so excited we couldn't stand it. Luckily we returned home without many other stops along the way, and we rushed with our treasure to our secret spot outside among the trees. We could be alone here.

Desi reached into the plastic bag and grabbed our prized possession. She held it up for us both to admire, and we knew it would be *just perfect*. Slowly she removed the outer carton, careful not to snag or loosen it while doing so.

Every superhero needs a trusty tool belt to get out of sticky situations, and we were about to have ours. We giggled in anticipation. Desi was going to make my belt first, then turn around and make her own. My heart skipped a beat as she began. I could see it coming together with each strand of our beautiful yarn weaving tighter and tighter together to form my very own instrument for crime fighting. Before I knew it, she had constructed a masterpiece that even Ms. Woman would have envied.

We jumped up and down from excitement and pride. We were real superheroes now, or at least I was. It was time to finish the task. Desi needed a belt that was just as snazzy. Grabbing the spool, I saw a faint and fleeting expression cross her face, that if I hadn't known her as well as I did, I might never have noticed. And then I was aware too. Our precious yarn was all but depleted, and she was left holding the remains. In her creative zeal, she had used it up on me. I stood guiltily wearing the combination of both our savings.

"We can share," I said, "…take turns or something."
I knew just as the words parted my lips that this was impossible. One small tug and our belt would be nothing but tatters, its magnificence a memory. She must have noticed its delicacy too, but more importantly my sorrowful face. "It's okay—one superhero belt will work for us both," she said. And looking into her eyes, I knew she meant it.

Two crime fighters made history that day—they fought every bad guy around while sharing one very special belt. We like to think it was, in fact, even more powerful when shared by two. This fragile belt was woven tightly through the strong bonds of friendship, and because of one sister's small sacrifice, it was destined never to deteriorate. Foregoing something so cherished to another made it invincible. It had powers that would never falter, and its creator was the real superhero.

* * *

Since the February 2005 release of our first CD, self-titled The 5 Browns, *we have traveled the world, bringing classical music to a wide variety of audiences. Our travels have taken us everywhere from large cities in Europe, Asia, and the United States to the small college towns in between. The following story takes place in the small town of Mason City, Iowa.*

HANK'S INN

BY MELODY BROWN

Iowa
March 2008

"Um…so I don't know how to put this, but I sort of get an icky feeling in my room."

The hotel clerk definitely didn't know how to answer my brother on that one. To understand why Ryan would say this to a perfect stranger, you'll have to step with us through the doors of Hank's Inn.

To tell you the truth, most of us had an "icky feeling" as we walked in. When the sign says "free cable and HBO," you know you're in for something. Most hotels like Hank's have their own little idiosyncrasies that really do make them "one of a kind." We try to avoid the neon-sign hotels, but sometimes it's all the concert hall can offer in a small town. In some cases, it's all the small town can offer.

When I first opened *my* door I felt a bit relieved. The carpet looked fairly new, anyway. I stepped further into my room when I heard Ryan limply remark down the hallway, "What in the world happened in here?"

Desi's uneasy laughter said it all. I came in as Ryan was taking a picture of his bomb explosion of a room. He obviously couldn't live in this, so he made his first trip to the front desk.

"Uh, so I don't know what happened to my room, but the mattress is up on its side propped against the table and, well, there's no sheets, or pillows, or anything. It looks like somebody was searching for something and tore apart the room." Neither the hotel clerk nor Ryan knew what had gone on in there, but both assumed that it must have been sketchy.

I can't imagine the look on Ryan's face a short while later when he opened the door to his newly upgraded honeymoon suite. He called us to take part in the exhibition.

It was the first time in our travels to hundreds of hotels where I found myself stepping *up* into a suite. "Well, you've got a stairway to honeymoon heaven; should be promising." I almost walked into the bed as I said it.

It was all at the craziest angles I'd ever seen. The whole room, come to think of it, was in opposition with itself. The bed's lower left corner was jutting into the doorway. A fake rock Jacuzzi tub took over the far right corner of the room. I couldn't tell whether the Jacuzzi was part of the bedroom or the partially walled-off bathroom; it squatted on shaggy carpet straddling both. The subtle touch of the stained khaki carpet against green curtains was breathtaking. But really, forget everything else; the bed was the main focus here. It took up the whole room at its angle near the door. The golden silk bedspread was most eye-catching; the stains directly reflected off the long mirrors of the headboard. That is, if you want to call that thing a headboard. About fifteen feet in length, it encompassed the entire room. Who needs just a headboard when you've got shelves, drawers, and mirrors? You didn't have to guess what you'd look like in the Jacuzzi; the immense mirrored headboard would take care of that. Come to think of it, obsessing over your hair in the reflection could drive one mad. Stand by the doorway, the closet, the table, or any part of the room and the headboard would reflect your decreasing self-esteem. The cherry on top was a thick-legged table adorned with giant silk hydrangeas. Massive dusty flowers were sure to give his honeymoon suite the perfect "finishing touch" of allergens.

"Well…good luck with that!" Our laughter trailed off as he closed the door.

Seven o'clock came pretty quickly for dinner. The rib joint next door looked appetizing enough, and before long we had barbecue sauce on our fingers. We joked over our dirty hands about our dirty rooms. Desi's first experience with her bathroom was with something brown and hairy on her toilet seat. Hoping it was a stain or crack, she began to wipe it off. I don't know which was better, the fact that it wiped off, or that it wasn't a stain. She went next to her bed, hoping to find comfort in her sheets after a long day of traveling. At least they *had* to have been washed, or so you'd think. She peeled back the sheets to find a mess of hair underneath. Sharing a bed with Goldy's numerous locks was anything but comforting. Though according to her, the remains weren't so "goldy."

Of course Ryan's room—excuse me, his *suite*—was the main topic of our dinner.

"You guys don't understand." He looked a little more serious. "I swear something bad happened in there."

We tried to restrain ourselves, although little bits of mockery were leaking out. He went on, "I don't know. I get this strange feeling, like maybe the furniture is all in strange positions to cover things up."

Gregory couldn't help jumping in. "Like there had been caution tape around the room? And the huge headboard-shelves-chest-of-drawers thing was covering up a massive blood stain?"

"…Yeah," Ryan said, looking a little more like his thoughts were surfacing in words.

Desi shushed us. "Wait, what do you mean?"

"Okay, well when I was taking a short nap, for instance, I had this strange dream. I never dream that I'm actually in my surroundings, but it's like I was standing next to myself, next to the bed I was sleeping in, taking in the strangeness of the room. I was moving back into myself, sleeping, when all of a sudden I looked up as someone jumped on the foot of the bed. A girl said, 'Hey!'"

He trailed off. "I woke up and there was no one there."

We looked at one another. "Freaky…."

Dinner ended on a somber note as we contemplated returning to our haunted hotel. Pulling up to the inn, we decided against parking at the back of the building by our rooms. That parking lot was much closer than having to walk those endless hallways inside, but we had our reasons.

"You didn't see that parking lot." Evidently one of us had. "It borders a field with a few flickering lights where old beat-up cars are parked next to rusted lawn furniture. I really think we should go through the front entrance."

We all had to agree when we saw it. That back lot could've been a scene right out of *Saw XXII*. I figured a man with a freaky saw could've jumped out any one of those abandoned cars. Going through the front entrance had one advantage: not being killed. Anyway, poor Ryan was in no rush to get back to his horror of a love shack.

While circling the parking lot we suggested that maybe he should just request a new room. "Just play it cool and casually ask if anything—I don't know—*bad* has happened in there."

Gregory, Desi, and I took off down the hallway, leaving our soon-to-be crazy brother standing at the front desk. He did have the lone moral support of trusty Deondra. Ryan's voice carried, so we stopped to listen from as far away as possible.

"Um, so I don't know how to put this, but I sort of get an icky feeling in my room. I can't help thinking that… well, did something bad happen in there?"

The hotel clerk looked at him sideways and raised an eyebrow.

Plowing ahead through her incredulity, he asked, "Have you ever seen the movie *1408*? You know, about the haunted hotel room?"

"Nope, I can't say that I have. But, um…I can go get my manager and ask her about your problem."

You'd think she'd try to hold back her sniggering as she walked a few feet into the pub that adjoined the hotel. A few seconds of silence passed before all we could hear were incredibly loud *roars* of laughter—multiple roars.

The manager came out, amused, as if this were the craziest thing she'd ever heard in all her years of working there.

"I can honestly tell you that this is a very safe hotel. Nothing bad has ever happened here."

Of course—that's what we all thought she would say. Ryan and Deon hurriedly joined us in the hallway with the clerk's words ringing in mockery: "Well, let us know what happens!"

A few minutes later I was huddling in my sheets when I got a random text message from Deon:

Well, I went to the bathroom in the dark a few times today, but now that it's night I turned on the light. I've been sitting on a stream of not-too-dried blood, and it's not from me!

Although we hadn't found any blood in Ryan's room, evidently there was plenty to spare in Deon's. If only this had been a clue to unlocking some murderous secret. Sadly the blood was only a sick vestige of the hotel's lack of sanitation.

I'm surprised any of us slept that night. When the lights went out I had to try incredibly hard to block out the fear. Thinking of beaches and cute cats, I swore that I WOULD NOT wake up to a dead girl jumping on my bed. Suddenly movies like *The Sixth Sense* were turning into reality. My sunny beach started morphing into a kid with a gunshot wound in his head walking through a wall, or the scene where the dead lady storms the kitchen with a slit throat and wrists.

"Sunny beaches…sunny beaches…sand between my sunburned toes…," I repeated to myself over and over. Cute cats were getting harder and harder to imagine. It was horrible that all I could think of while alone in that dark room were the scariest scenes from the scariest movies. I started wishing I had never seen those movies. And on top of it all was guilt. I had once gone to a church devotional where the speaker, a leader in the LDS church by the name of Dallin H. Oaks, had warned us against just this. He cautioned that in viewing shady stuff, the unwanted things tend to stay with you. He likened it to eating spoiled food. The body will fight back and try to get rid of what's making you sick, but the mind has no way of "vomiting back filth."

"Once recorded, it will always remain subject to recall, flashing its [tainted] images across your mind and drawing you away from the wholesome things in life."

In other words, the mind literally keeps regurgitating bad things you've seen, never able to fully purge the memory. It's always stored somewhere deep in the layers upon layers of trash you've been exposed to throughout life. Suddenly I could hear him saying "I told you so" when the lights went out. My scary-scene flashbacks were attacking me uncontrollably. The only antidote I could think of in the middle of the night was turning on the TV, technically the source of my problems. After a while of filling up for future flashback sessions of the crass and stupid, I finally fell asleep.

Morning was a relief; thank goodness I couldn't remember any dreams of dead girls or gunshot wounds. I found myself elated to leave the room for the day. Thirteen hours would be enough to rid myself of the fear. Even the fifty-mile-per-hour subzero winds would somehow chap my mind into numbness.

Our day did have an end, though. After the concert was over, our last night in the beloved inn was upon us. We had only nine hours to endure before we could move on in hopes of a better home the following day. The "after-concert high" sank a bit as we crossed the hotel threshold. It plummeted as we walked the *Green Mile* hallways and one by one lost our comrades along the way. "Good night" and "Remember, tomorrow morning at nine" were the final verses of our five-times-repeated chant. I passed Deondra on the fourth time, since my door was the last and farthest.

"Good night," she said without thinking.

"Good night."

"Remember, tomorrow morning at...oh, that's just great. My key doesn't work."

I wasn't walking the Bataan Death March again. I left Deondra to endure it on her own. I couldn't figure out which was worse, trudging the hallways or stepping back into the remains of scary-movie flashbacks. The musty smell of the room upon opening the door brought all the fear back to the surface. A part of me lingered in the hallway in support of Deondra, but ultimately the hope of clean sheets and sound sleep pushed me further into my room.

The nine-hour sentence eventually ended with the morning's dreary light. The usual "you were late" wasn't heard when we met up to leave. Everyone was on time, an incredibly rare achievement. You'd think we were on another "after-concert high" the way we were loading the suitcases. We could've robbed a bank with our getaway-car driving. It was sheer triumph. As Hank's Inn became smaller and smaller out the rear windshield, the cheers were so loud that we couldn't hear Deon trying to talk. She must've started her "Guys! Seriously, you *have* to hear this…" at least a dozen times. Finally, Hank's Inn was out of sight.

"So you know how my key didn't work last night? Well, I went to the front desk, and the lady was actually really nice this time. She asked how the concert went and said she'd seen us in the newspaper. She wished she could've gotten off her shift to come. We were talking for a bit when I was handed my key. I told her 'thanks' and started to walk away, when she offered to walk me to my door. I said I was fine, but she insisted. So we kept talking for a while in those hallways when we finally reached my room. I was in the middle of saying good night when she cut me off with, 'MAKE SURE YOU BOLT YOUR DOOR.' Her expression completely changed. She was dead serious. I was kind of surprised and said, 'Oh, I know, I usually do.' 'WELL, YOU JUST MAKE SURE YOU DO.' Right then I knew that bad stuff *has* happened there!"

We knew it. The place had a shady past. Of course, we didn't know what kind of shady past. Might we be overreacting about the manager warning us to bolt our doors? I started imagining Ryan as a psychic in the honeymoon suite tapping into another realm and seeing that murdered girl, her bloodstains under his enormous headboard. My mind exploded at the possibilities of things that could've happened in that room of his. Maybe ignorance was bliss, but one thing's for sure: We're never going back there again.

The next night, even though I was snuggled in the clean bed of my new hotel home, I still couldn't rid myself of Hank and his morbid inn. I dragged the ghost of it into my cheery room once the lights went out.

"Sunny beaches, sand between my sunburned toes, Persian kittens with pouty faces, babies laughing…"

No matter how much I repeated my mantra, it didn't purge the memory of that place and the endless scary movie scenarios I'd conjured up there.

"Sunny beaches…Beeeeeeeeeaches…Freaky dead girl…Hank's Inn."

I imagined noises and dark figures in the corner. I couldn't let the TV be my safe haven again. On the brink of tears, I must have subconsciously mustered the strength to contend.

An old prayer my mom used to say growing up as a Baptist popped into my head.

"Now I lay me down to sleep. I pray the Lord my soul to keep."

I slowly found myself drifting.

"My soul to keep…. My soul to keeeeeeeeep…."

Thank goodness the mind holds onto the good things as well.

* * *

Wisdom is hard to define. Usually the old among us possess it. Sometimes the rest of us obtain fragments of it, and we turn it in our hands before it somehow slips through our fingers. What was it that I knew then? How did I get through that difficult time? When you meet somebody wise, you know it. They have been taught things that we haven't learned yet.

VICTORIA

BY DESIRAE BROWN

Ohio
February 2008

Rarely do you have the opportunity to know what people really think of you. Sometimes you *think* you really want to know, sometimes you even guess. Guessing isn't that healthy, as most of us probably have a weaker self-esteem than we think. We just end up tearing ourselves down trying to project upon our minds what others are thinking. Not a good game. Every once in a while we may have a good day, and suddenly we are a superhero or supermodel walking down the street, but those days are few, and sadly, way too far between. Usually you just don't want to know.

Like the time all five of us were attending Juilliard when an article in *The New York Times* came out about our family. It was a strange day, kind of like a good dream and a bad dream mixed into one. The day started by our reading the story after we woke up, followed by great feelings of relief that the writer and editors were kind to us. That was the good part. Then we had to go to school and face everyone we knew. A lot of Juilliard students subscribe to the paper, so a lot of copies were floating around. A select few friends were excited for us, jumping up and down and clapping to see their friends on the cover of the Arts section. But everyone else seemed, well, a little less than thrilled.

After trying to do some quiet celebrating in the school lobby with those few friends, I felt a strange sense of paranoia setting in, like people were watching me. I slowly started to look around. Students were huddled in small groups whispering amongst themselves and looking our way. All the little cliques had come together, some of them still holding the Arts section in their hands. There was the Russian clique, visibly angered by the seeming injustice, sending us obvious cutting glares. And the virtuoso group, doing a better job of seeming nonchalant, but staring nonetheless. And I could see the smokers with their cocky smiles outside on the plaza. Even with the floor-to-ceiling glass between us, I could see them enjoying the show. At that moment I did *not* want to know what everyone was thinking. I was only too afraid that what they were thinking might be what I was thinking. And I was afraid it might be true. Maybe we weren't good enough.

The stares and whispers continued all day. The gossiping that we weren't included in, but could clearly see, began to feel like resentment. It became nearly unbearable. I almost wanted to take the article back so that everyone could feel better, and I could go back to being invisible. When that school day was over, we had considerably fewer friends. It was kind of a refining process. The true friends that remained are close friends to this day. They have been to our weddings, let us cry on their shoulders (and cried on ours in return), and supported us at our performances. They've even let us subject them to the torture of being interviewed on our behalf. Now *that's* a sign of true friendship.

After that experience, I cared far less what people thought of me, or my talent, or my value as a performer or a person. Even many years later, when we started recording albums and touring the country and the world, I tried not to let it get to me. We've been blessed with many good reviews and some not-so-good reviews. All in all, I've realized it only matters if our audiences as a whole like what they hear, if we can touch their hearts. If we can touch people, then it doesn't matter what all the critics, professional or otherwise, have to say.

There was one very special audience member we met once. She came up to us with her mother in tow. Hardly a critic, she described herself as a fan. She couldn't have been more than seventeen. She had a pallor to her skin, and fatigue showed in her body language. I noticed she had a tube coming out from underneath her shirt that was attached to a pack secured around her waist. As she spoke to us there was a feverish, glistening excitement in her eyes. Her name was Victoria. She apologized for her weakness and explained that she had cancer. She said that she had all of our CDs and loved music in general, but found classical to be her favorite. It helped to calm her. She had been through many rounds of chemotherapy and had suffered a lot of pain. Victoria explained that when the pain got unbearable she'd play the music from our CDs, and it helped to distract her until it passed or until the medication would begin to course through her body.

Then she started talking about something that Greg had said during the interview portion of our concert. (At the start of the second half of some of our concerts, we leave a few minutes to take questions from the audience.) At this particular concert, Greg had been asked if we felt that we were proselytizing for our church when we travel the world and speak to people. He explained that, no, we don't proselytize for our church, but that we *do* try to bring good things into people's lives. We want to give parents and kids out there an alternative to the questionable music and entertainment saturating our culture. He also described how we hoped to be good examples in the way we dress and speak. We also hope to be an example of brothers and sisters who love and support one another. And mostly, we want to bring the joy of good music into the lives of others.

Victoria told us that what we were trying to do, and what Greg had said, was important, and not to forget it.

"I just want to let you know," Victoria started, "that I don't know how I would get through this time in my life without your music. I thank God for your music and that you have shared it with me. I almost didn't come tonight. I felt so sick. But I just couldn't miss it. And during the concert, if the pain started to get too terrible, I would pray, and then you would start to play some of my favorite music, and the pain would lessen so I could enjoy it. Thank you for a night away from the pain."

When she said that, I didn't know what to say. I felt ashamed, overwhelmed, and undeserving as she shared her life with such honesty. Why was she thanking us? I didn't deserve it. Whatever she felt that we gave her was nothing compared to the example of strength she was to us. We had a hero in our midst. There, in the crowded lobby with people surrounding us and yelling over us, Victoria used all her strength to stand and thank *us*. All this to make *us* feel good, to let us know how we'd helped her. I needed to thank *her*, not the other way around.

Victoria could have been bitter and angry at what life had dealt her. At the prime of her life, her dreams were being cut short. But she chose to cling to the beautiful things in life. We also clung to the beautiful things by choosing a life in classical music. Undeserving as we may be, we knew we had met a superhero that night. She couldn't save her body from the ravages of cancer, but maybe the beautiful things could help heal her spirit.

I know we walk the earth with angels in our midst, and when you meet one, it changes your life forever. I know that the praise of critics is not what I want in order to define my life, but rather the hearts, one by one, that I may be able to touch for good, just as Victoria touched mine.

*　*　*

I figured, "I'm a pretty tough guy, I can play through this," so I
continued even though my better judgment was suggesting I stop.

SUPERSHOES AND THE PURPLE BLUR

BY GREGORY BROWN

Alpine, Utah, and Some Airport
Winter 2007

I hate photo shoots. Let me just get that out there right now. Every time I step in front of a camera for one of these full-day events, it inevitably ends up being one of the worst days of my life. I get all awkward and uncomfortable, and I always end up having severe struggles with my surroundings.

If they turn on a fan to give us the ole sexy-windblown look, it dries out my eyes, and I can't keep them open. Imagine how much fun it is for me to try picking a good shot for an album cover when my eyes are closed in all of them. Then there are the outside shots. There's no fan, which is great, but then there's the sun to deal with. If it's too bright or bright-gray and overcast, again I can't keep my dang eyes open for more than a second. Once I even woke up on the morning of a photo shoot and found that I had scratched my cornea while I slept (probably due to the rapid eye movement induced by my photo-shoot nightmares), and I had to go around all day wearing a freakin' eye patch. Nothing quite says "Yeeargh, I'm ready fer me close-up" like a nice eye patch.

The one saving grace about these photo shoots, however, is the free stuff that you come away with. If stuff gets a little damaged during the shoot or if the stylist had to cut the tags off for some reason, it's all yours. One of the shoots we did outside for our second album included these sweet purple suede Pumas. I was disappointed that the stylist chose them for Ryan and not me, but my spirits rebounded after the shoot when Ryan decided he didn't really want them. Of course, that left me as their only claimant, and I was more than happy to take over.

The following winter, I stayed at my parents' home for a couple of weeks over the holidays. As I packed the stuff I wanted to take, I decided I'd grab these super-sexy purple Pumas for "just in case." They might come in handy in the event of a "dress to impress" scenario. I was right too.

These awesome shoes did come in handy while I was home—just not quite the way I expected. I ended up reaching for them not to show off my style on a hot date, not because my sisters dressed me for a cool TV appearance, and no, not even as one of the many pairs of shoes I tried on in front of the mirror in my mom's closet (don't start rumors now, I'm only kidding); I reached for them, instead, as my solution to a predicament posed by my bishop: "church basketball tournament this week!"

I was almost forced to play and considered it my duty to answer my church's pleas (more or less) for the donation of my sick skills, but I had totally forgotten to bring my basketball shoes from my house a half hour away. So my choices were these: waste an hour driving home and back, sport my dress shoes, wear my everyday shoes that were starting to fall apart, slip on my snow boots, or…yup, those purple beasts themselves. I'm sure you've guessed by now which choice I went with. The big problem, though, was not that they were flashy and ridiculously attractive, but that they were a full size too small.

So I'm on the court—practically scoring at will in these dazzling plum treads, which hugged my feet in a rather intimate way—and the defense couldn't even figure out what hit them. All they could see was a purple blur zooming past them to the hoop.

That lasted for about five minutes.

Gradually, minute by minute, I slowed down, and the defense could see that the purple blur was just a lanky guy in metrosexual shoes. At about the same time that the laughter set in throughout the gym, I realized that I couldn't feel my feet. No, no, I take that back—*all* I could feel were my feet, specifically the throbbing pain in my considerably curled big toes. I figured, "I'm a pretty tough guy, I can play through this," so I continued even though my better judgment suggested I stop.

I got slower and slower, and before I knew it, the opposition was scoring on *me* at will (well, "at will" is slightly generous). I soldiered through it until I was walking like Mini-Me from *Austin Powers*. By the time I got home and removed the wretched mauve vices from my feet, my two big toenails were the same color as the culprits that killed them (except with a hint of the color *blood*).

Well, to make a long story a little shorter, imagine a can of Campbell's tomato soup. Now take this can of soup and begin removing the lid with a can opener. Once it's opened just enough, pour the soup into a bowl and enjoy. Now, take this same story and substitute the words *toe* for *can*, *blood* for *tomato soup*, *toenail* for *lid*, *small knife* for *can opener*, *bathtub* for *bowl*, and *weep uncontrollably* for *enjoy*, and then you've pretty much got the picture.

As for now, if my toes followed the same seasons as the trees, you could say that it's autumn time in my shoes, and the leaves are changing color quite exquisitely. A barren winter should be along shortly, and I very much look forward to the splendor of spring.

*　*　*

The heartbreaking events that followed were a bit of a blur, but I vaguely remember the words "Oh, no" and "Gregory, I'm so sorry" as I gazed down at the grisly scene.

There's this piece I learned a while back called "Superstar Etude No.1." I'll often play it at the end of the first half of our concerts to wake up any narcoleptics who escaped into classical dreamland for a minute or two—bobbing their unconscious little heads along with the pretty music. The piece is a bit of an homage to Mr. "Great Balls of Fire" himself, Jerry Lee Lewis, so it fittingly includes a few of his piano techniques that are, well, unusual for classical musicians, to say the least. It was composed by A. J. Kernis, a respected classical composer, but it's more or less a fusion of modern classical dissonance and rock and roll.

When I first saw the sheet music and started trying to make sense of it, my reaction was: "Wait, I have to do *what*?" and with each successive turn of the page, I grew more and more dumbfounded. "I have to play with my elbows?" "I have to play with my feet?" "I have to shout 'whoa baby' at the top of my lungs?" I soon got over my fears of screaming at old people and kids from the piano bench and decided that this could be a lot of fun. Plus, it was an opportunity to show off my favorite black Converse hi-tops while throwing them up onto the keys.

Anyway, I had quite the traumatic experience at the airport one day, and those incredibly attractive superstar shoes were basically massacred. Yeah, I know what you're thinking—"not that; anything but the performance shoes"—and I have to say, I couldn't agree more. But before I can expect you to drop whatever you're doing and aid me in the composition of a lovingly fitting obituary for my faithful canvas friends, I better first give you the full report of their untimely and tragic demise.

We had just stepped off the plane after a long and tiring flight, and my feet were feeling unusually content. This, of course, was a pleasant surprise, considering that airplanes typically transform my least attractive appendages into nigh more than swollen, flattened sausages. Needless to say, I was quite proud of my trusty black Converse, and I sported them so on my way to claim my baggage.

We arrived at baggage claim only to find that they were experiencing difficulty in locating our stuff, so while we waited for them to retrieve it, we figured: "What better way to pass the time than by filling our tiny bellies with a good old, traditional American meal." After ordering our Big Macs and fries, we took particular care in acquiring a more-than-sufficient number of ketchup packets for enhancing the savory flavor of the processed, synthetic goodness. My dad was especially excited about the prospect of this kingly feast, and in a moment of haste he gave his little packet a good squeeze before aptly removing its corner, causing an entirely different escape route for the liquid within. The heartbreaking events that followed were a bit of a blur, but I vaguely remember the words "Oh, no" and "Gregory, I'm so sorry" as I gazed down at the grisly scene.

My poor high-topped little buddies never knew what hit them, and I don't think they'll ever fully recover from the bloody mess—much less grace the piano keys onstage. I think they must have ended up absorbing more of that hellish garnish than was on all six of our Big Macs combined. We did all that we could to revive them, but I guess it was just their time to go. May you rest in peace, my beloved Superstar Shoes.

* * *

I know what I like in a performer. Some people in the industry call it the "X factor" or "that special something." I think it's generosity. Great performers open up to an audience and bare their soul. These special artists aren't thinking of what the audience is thinking of them. They are completely lost in the moment, in a memory, in a sound, in a feeling. Seeing such a performer is so satisfying because you walk away feeling what they were feeling.

THE BEST CONCERT EVER

BY DESIRAE BROWN

**Philadelphia
2006**

I remember the feeling vividly. My heart was skipping and my palms were sweating. We couldn't have been on the air yet because the producer had said that as long as the floor-to-ceiling black screen was down, we weren't being filmed. We could visualize the cameras and studio audience, though. We knew what was waiting for us. The five of us were seated at five Steinways, smiling and giggling from nervous energy and excitement. I must have looked nervous because Gregory started singing Britney Spears quietly while dancing at his piano bench to make me laugh. Whenever one of us stopped smiling and stared off into space long enough to consider what was actually happening, he started singing again. I looked around the set and felt like I had shrunk into my television screen. It was so familiar, yet bigger than I had imagined. So this was what it felt like to be on the set of *The Tonight Show with Jay Leno*. Jay Leno, the guy on TV, was one of those common, comfortable things that seeped into my everyday life. I grew up laughing with him late at night. I never dreamed that I would be sitting *behind* that screen one day. Never.

The rehearsal had gone well that day. We walked around the set as the producer gave us a tour. She was brisk, competent, and to the point, the kind that doesn't waste time. She explained that they had installed a camera in the ceiling over the performance space so that viewers could get an overhead shot of all the pianos. The crew was excited about that shot and had hurried to arrange it for our performance. She said they had been intending to install the camera for years and now had an excuse. I guess if you ever watch the show and see a band from overhead, that camera's there in part because of us.

After the tour, we returned to our dressing rooms and nervously dressed for the show. It was a big and busy day. Our first album was being released, and we were about to perform on *The Tonight Show*. While waiting for our "places" call, we heard a knock on our dressing room door. The small room was already packed with managers, record executives, and publicists, so I wondered where one more could possibly fit. And then Jay Leno walked in, wearing blue jeans and a denim shirt with Mickey Mouse embroidered into the pocket. He smiled, shook our hands, and cracked jokes. We got nervous after that.

I usually get nervous anticipating the unknown, so I was relieved when the time came to walk onstage behind the black screen. As I took my place at the piano and looked around at my brothers and sisters and saw how excited they were, I started to forget about being nervous. As much as I felt like I didn't know what I was doing, I wanted to enjoy this. We laughed in whispers, cracked jokes, and danced to Gregory's impersonation of pop music superstars to get us pumped up. That's what we were doing behind the black screen, and what we most often do before walking onstage for a concert.

Eventually the cue came, the screen quickly rose up into the ceiling, and we started playing. Before I had time to realize what was happening, the audience was clapping and we were bowing. We joined Jay Leno in front of the pianos, and he announced the end of the show. We shook his hand and chatted while the credits were rolling, and then it was over. Five minutes, and it was over. That was our first live television show.

Over the next couple of weeks, we became practiced at performing on live TV. We learned how to clip the mic-pack onto our waists at the back and then string the cord up underneath our clothes to place the tiny microphone at our collars. We learned what "teaser" and "hard ending" meant. We realized that camera crews are made up of really cool guys, and that making friends always makes the experience better, not to mention that then they'll have your back. And it's usually better to look at your interviewer rather than to stare blankly into the camera. We also learned that we hated earpieces and hearing ourselves back through monitors. I guess television shows use them so you can hear yourself better. We'd almost rather throw ourselves under a train than use a monitor, because when we use one, that's basically what we're doing. Those monitors sabotage the performance because we can't hear anything but our individual pianos. In other words, we can't hear the other four pianists with whom we should be playing. We're classical musicians and only trust our own ears.

With the release of our second album, we learned that we had been invited to perform on some other TV shows, including *The Martha Stewart Show.* Secretly, it's more fun to perform on shows that we actually kind of watch. Well, *I* watch *The Martha Stewart Show.* My brothers watch ESPN.

I was excited to play on the show but was unprepared for a request that came from the show's producers. Could one of us teach Martha how to play one of our pieces on air?

They really wanted to see Martha at one of our pianos playing with us. When the five of us heard about the request, everyone claimed "not it." We took a vote, and I was the one elected to teach Martha something to play. Now, if you don't know already, Martha Stewart knows how to do everything. E-v-e-r-y-t-h-i-n-g. I've seen guests on her show who are experts in their field stand corrected by her. Visions of trying to teach Martha Stewart to do *anything* were beginning to really freak me out. I had my dad call the producer to find out how comfortable Martha felt at the piano. Did she have any training? Had she played a note in her life? The producer said he didn't know, but would get back to us.

When we were shown to our dressing rooms backstage at the show, we knew we were someplace special. This place looked nothing like any other backstage we had seen. It felt like we had stumbled into a five-star hotel suite in the middle of a soundstage. The warm, freshly baked sticky buns left for us on the coffee table suggested that there was a five-star chef around too. After we dropped our change of clothes in the suite, we walked onto the set for the sound- and camera-check. The set was amazing, the largest indoor open space I think I've seen in New York City. True to what you would expect from Martha Stewart, everything was immaculate and breathtaking. Usually the sets look great on TV, but when you walk up close to the backdrops in person, things look a little, well, worn. But not at Martha Stewart's show. All the flowers were fresh and there were chefs walking in with trays of piping hot food to be used on the show. It happened to be spring, and we felt like we had been dropped into an Easter fantasy courtesy of Martha Stewart.

Post-soundcheck, we lounged in the suite, munched on gourmet treats, and changed for the show. Then I remembered that I had to teach Martha to play something at the piano. I slipped out of the suite and began wandering around the set, looking for a producer I recognized. After dodging trees, cookies, and plants being brought in, I tapped a producer on the shoulder.

"I'm sorry to bother you," I broke in, "but I know I'm supposed to teach Martha something to play on the show, and

I was just wondering if you happened to know what her skill level is. You know, does she play a little, or maybe a lot, or just 'Chopsticks'?"

"Oh yes, I've just spoken with her," he replied, "and she really hasn't ever played before. I hope that's not a problem...."

"Oh no, no. That shouldn't be a problem. I've got some ideas. Thanks so much."

I smiled and maneuvered my way back to the dressing room. Once the door was shut I announced, "Guys, guess what? You know how I'm supposed to teach Martha how to play something? Well, apparently she doesn't play at all."

"Oooh, shoot!" Gregory clapped his hands once then threw his head back and laughed, "Glad I'm not the one teaching her. What are you gonna do?"

"I don't know."

Then everyone started throwing out suggestions of pieces we could play and what part she had a chance of learning in a few seconds on air. Everyone was talking over everyone else, so there were a few minutes of mayhem.

"Okay, okay," I finally broke in. "Maybe I'll just teach her the bottom two notes of *In the Hall of the Mountain King*. You know, the notes at the opening. Yeah, that's what I'll do.... Then you guys just start playing when she starts to get it, okay?"

"Just, like, start playing whenever...?" Melody asked, suspicious and uncertain. This couldn't possibly be a good plan.

"Hey, good luck with that," Ryan chimed in, turning back to his computer screen.

What to teach Martha Stewart on air was mostly what I was thinking about as we walked out to chat with her before we performed *Rhapsody in Blue* for our segment. That, and the clashing shades of purple that Martha and I had unfortunately decided to wear. I'm sure this didn't cross the minds of most viewers, but I'm pretty certain it crossed Martha's mind as we greeted each other. I saw it flit across her eyes at the same time that I had visions of our clashing purples side by side at the piano bench. I hoped this wouldn't affect our relationship. We proceeded like troopers, clashing purples and all. The performance went pretty well, and the live studio audience was perfectly timed for cheering. Then Martha strolled over to our pianos and asked if she could join us. She had heard that one of us was going to teach her how to play! The cheers erupted.

I jumped up from my piano bench and offered her a seat. She looked a little disoriented as she took in the eighty-eight keys and then looked back at me for assistance. I set her left middle finger on a low B note and her right middle finger on an F-sharp, and had her switch off, playing each one in a steady rhythm. She was doing so well that I thought I could teach her to play the next two notes, and thus play more of the piece, but her expression turned a little frantic, so I aborted that plan. She went back to just the first two notes and started bobbing her head. As she did, my brothers and sisters started playing the opening bars of *In the Hall of the Mountain King*, by Edvard Grieg. Her face lit up and somehow a miracle happened. Martha Stewart was playing with four concert pianists, live on her show. After about twenty seconds, the magic was over, and the audience's applause broke in with a coordinated, rhythmic precision that has taken the five of us years to master.

Martha Stewart rose from the piano bench, probably for the first and last time, and then said she had an announcement. Huh, I thought. The producers had gone through every step of the show with us, and hadn't said anything about an announcement.

"Well, I hear that your favorite band is Coldplay," she started, "and we found out that Coldplay is giving their last U.S. appearance tonight in Philadelphia. Sooo, we have arranged for the five of you to be taken in a limo to Philadelphia, and have five tickets for you for tonight's sold-out concert!"

We were so surprised to have something like this happen, and on TV no less, that we started jumping and laughing. When we eventually looked back at the footage, I guess it was kind of embarrassing, all the jumping and crazy expressions, but it was totally worth it. Coldplay! Every single one of us had all their albums but had never heard them live. Hearing a band live is the true test of their talent.

Back in the suite, I realized just how exhausted I was. My head was pounding and I felt shaky. The two weeks preceding the *Martha Stewart* appearance had been heavily scheduled with concerts and early morning television appearances, and as usual the strain was taking its toll on my body. The nausea was building, and I wished I could feel better so I could really enjoy the concert that night. I just figured I had pushed myself for work so many times before that I owed it to myself to push on for *fun*. To be honest, sometimes amid the craziness, life can get really hard. Sometimes we miss our spouses. Sometimes our health doesn't hold up. Sometimes we feel we can't learn and memorize the music fast enough for deadlines. And sometimes I can't sleep because of it all. Sometimes the pressure just gets to us.

I remember having a day like this and breaking down in rehearsal. I had put my arms up on the fallboard of the piano and just started sobbing, while the rest of my siblings looked on in silence, worry, and empathy. They let me cry for a while. Then, with my head still buried in the piano, I started to hear the strains of one of my favorite Coldplay songs, "Fix You," being played on one of the pianos. Greg likes to play Coldplay songs at the piano sometimes on breaks during our rehearsals. He'll start playing, and then one by one we'll start singing along in the harmonies from the album. One of us might even get out our cell phone and wave it in the air as though we were at a concert, or we'll just put one hand each in the air and sway to the music. Gregory started singing the words, then all the others joined in:

"When you try your best but you don't succeed
When you get what you want but not what you need
When you feel so tired but you can't sleep
Stuck in reverse
The tears come streaming down your face
When you lose something you can't replace
When you love someone but it goes to waste
Could it be worse
Lights will guide you home
And ignite your bones
And I will try to fix you."

Soon I felt arms around me, and I realized Melody was next to me on my piano bench. Then one by one everyone came to hug me, except Gregory, who was still playing at the piano. Then he couldn't stand it and came over too. Singing *a capella*, with their arms around me in a group hug, we all started swaying to the music and laughing and crying. Ever since then, "Fix You" has kind of become our anthem. Whenever anyone is sad or discouraged, we'll start singing it, and somehow we always feel better. I guess that's the gift of good music.

And so a few hours later, we found ourselves in a limo, leaving the traffic of New York City for a stretch of highway leading to Philly. Some of us slept on the drive while intermittently exclaiming over the craziness of the day.

I can't tell you how excited we were to hear Coldplay. Even if I tried, you probably wouldn't understand. Well, maybe I'll try.

At the Coldplay concert, our expectations were pretty high. At the top of the show, somebody came out to announce that Chris Martin, the lead singer, was sick and had gone to the doctor to get a cortisone shot that day. He had thought about canceling, but couldn't bear to disappoint us, the fans. I was already a little disappointed, and thought we wouldn't get a strong performance. I was totally wrong. I've rarely been so blown away by a performance of any kind, classical or otherwise. Chris Martin gave so much to the audience. He threw himself into every song, every word, every phrase; and he kept this incredible energy up the entire concert. He never exposed the immense fatigue he must have been feeling, being ill at the end of a tour. I will never forget that. At times, in my own performances, I think of Chris Martin and the force he put into that show. If I'm tired, or feeling lazy, I remind myself that if Chris Martin can do it, I should expect at least that much of myself. I owe that much to every audience.

Sometimes I think performers can be selfish and hold back a little bit for themselves, or maybe not truly expose everything. In classical music, there can be a tendency for performers to play for *themselves*, not necessarily for the audience. I've seen some classical performers not even acknowledge the audience. They walk out, look straight at the floor or at their instrument, play, then walk off without even glancing, much less bowing, to the audience. In a live performance there needs to be reciprocity.

There was a superstition at Juilliard that after watching somebody perform, you could tell a lot about his or her personality. It was almost like you could know people in a way that would normally take years by watching and hearing them play. I think there may be a little truth to it. In many ways I think you *can* tell if a person is generous and warm, or selfish and egotistical (and a lot more in between) by the way he or she plays. We've known a lot of musicians, and this "theory" holds up pretty well.

Sometimes I'll think of myself as a performer and wonder, am I warm or am I selfish? Do I help people feel comfortable, or do I push them away? Am I a show-off, or am I humble and honest? If I can emulate qualities of wonderful, caring, giving people and develop them in myself, then maybe those qualities will come across in the music I play. I hope so. I hope I can be like Chris Martin, and Yo-Yo Ma, and Bryan Luch, and Renée Fleming, and Leonard

Bernstein. I want to fully give of myself, on the stage and off. And it's crazy how you learn these things. You may start out as a kid playing the piano, become a professional classical musician, find yourself on *The Tonight Show*, be given tickets to Coldplay by Martha Stewart, and end up wanting to be like Chris Martin while playing classical music.

* * *

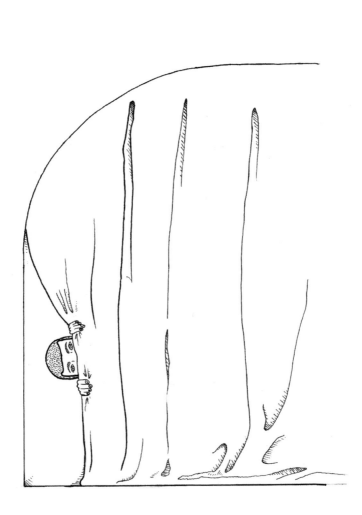

College Bulletin:

"Recently there have been some unusual muggings in the area, and students are to take precautions while walking the streets. Be careful and don't be out at late hours of the night. Thank you."

GOT MUGGED?

BY RYAN BROWN

New York City
Spring 2006

It was two-thirty on a Saturday night, and I knew that walking home from my friend's dorm was not going to be easy. We had just finished talking about how to get past life's challenges, and my eyes felt heavy. I said good night, and as I was leaving the building, I saw a few people talking outside in a somewhat intoxicated fashion. I walked by in a hurry to avoid running into their in-depth conversation about their favorite brands of beer. Since they didn't attack me as I passed, I breathed a sigh of relief.

As I was approaching the street corner at the end of the block I saw a suspicious-looking guy standing idly, wearing a big, baggy white shirt and jeans, a black puffy jacket, and a New York Yankees cap that still had the size sticker on the bill. He couldn't have been more than eighteen years old. I was nineteen at the time and felt a little intimidated by this guy because I had to walk by him on the sidewalk, and he looked much bigger than I was. Then I remembered the school bulletin I had seen about some recent muggings. After these things crossed my mind, I forced myself to think that I was just overreacting, and that I should walk confidently past.

As I came within five feet of the man, I avoided eye contact so as to not provoke him in any way. After I had quickly passed, I heard a scratching "thump-thump-thump" sound on the pebbly pavement as if someone were running from across the street toward me. I looked to my right in panic as I saw a tall, unfamiliar man sprinting at me, getting ready to pounce. I didn't have time to do anything but duck as he jumped on me. "Pow!" I felt an incredible hit on my back, and my breath was knocked out of me. Somehow still on my two feet, and trying to keep my legs in place, I felt hard hits on my neck and head, causing me to become discombobulated. He got about six hits in before I realized what was happening, and automatically, I started doing the unthinkable. I was a bit dizzy, in pain, and disoriented, but knowing my movements were strained because I had a backpack on didn't stop me from trying to defend myself. Clenching my right fist and spinning around as if to hit this man, I somehow threw him off of his rhythm. He jumped away from me and started running back across the street.

I checked my pockets and found my phone missing. I figured the man who jumped me had gone for my wallet but got my phone instead. I was relieved—but I couldn't let go of the disturbing feeling that my phone was gone. I saw two more thugs who must've been part of the same group pick it up off of the pavement. Both of them, to my astonishment, started laughing hysterically while walking down the street. Something about not having my phone, and the two of them laughing as they opened and closed it, really started annoying me. I wanted to run them down and get my phone back. I couldn't just stand there and watch them walk away like that. It was a worthless phone—the kind you get for free with a two-year plan. But believe it or not, it did cross my mind that I had just finished putting all 200 of my contacts back in after losing them along with my old phone. It would just be way too embarrassing to ask everybody for their numbers again, so I wanted to avoid it at all costs.

I threw off my backpack and ran those two kids down. While running, I was thinking one thing and one thing only:

"I know I'm a fast runner, and I'll catch these guys." Running down that street made me feel like the Flash—you know, that old comic book hero back in the day—because I was running at such incredible speeds and saving the world from—wait––cell phone thieves? Okay, maybe not the cell phone part, but the running was getting me somewhere. In about half a block I was leaping-distance from the kid with my phone. The thought of pouncing on him crossed my mind, but I realized this probably wouldn't be a smart thing to do in addition to the smart things I'd already done that night, such as running down strange kids that could easily have knives or guns. He must have seen how close I was because he threw my phone down on the street and kept running. I stopped, picked it up, walked back to the street corner, and picked up my backpack. There was now a cop on the other side of the street and I ran to his car. I told him what had happened, and he took out his radio and called for backup. Literally two minutes later—and I kid you not—there were over five cop cars patrolling the streets for four young men. Sirens were echoing everywhere.

All but five minutes later, a police SUV pulled up and a woman inside told me to get in the car. I was confused and thought that I was getting arrested now for something. I closed the door and the man driving said, "Can you identify?"

I said, "Do what?"

Again he asked, more forcefully, "Can you identify the suspects?!"

"Um, maybe...."

"We picked up four men on the streets and need you to be 100 percent sure who you identify as the men that attacked you. Can you do that?"

"Um...yeah," I said in a more confident voice, but now I felt totally unsure if I remembered what the guys looked like. I was scared, and I didn't want to send some random guys to jail.

The SUV stopped on the street, and I could see two cops guarding four guys in handcuffs. The man driving asked me, "Are those any of the men that attacked you?"

"I think maybe all four of them, but I'm not sure...."

That's not what the cop wanted to hear. He wanted a *yes* or *no* and was putting pressure on me, making it harder to decide. I then complained to him in an irritated voice, "I can't really tell when they're so far away. I can barely see any of their faces. Can we get closer or something?"

"No, against police laws. We've had problems with suspects threatening the people who accused them. We have to keep our distance so they can't make out faces."

I gulped and stopped complaining. With my face so fair and my hair so red, really anybody could spot me from a thousand feet away.

He then said, "It's risky even to roll down your window, but you should be fine to do so."

I had no choice but to roll it down because the windows in the SUV were so tinted.

I could finally see the faces of the four kids who were in handcuffs, but it was still hard to remember, because everything had happened so incredibly fast.

The pressure was on. Making sure I wasn't picking the wrong people was a hard and nerve-racking thing to do. My heart was pounding, and after a long minute, I decided to pick all four of the guys they had in handcuffs on the sidewalk. When I said they were the ones, the driver rolled up my window and pressed the gas hard to reach the station quickly so I could tell the police department my horrific experience. They wanted to know everything, down to the street names and where and when it happened. They wrote all this stuff down on paper and mapped out the whole scene with arrows, street names, and diagrams. They even asked me how many cars were on the street. It was crazy. I felt like I was on one of those cool *Law & Order* shows because everything was so unreal.

After they finished questioning me, I called Melody and Greg to let them know what had just happened. They freaked out and got mad at me for waking them up. They told me not to be walking back home at three in the morning and to get a cab if I'm ever out that late. I agreed. At this point in life, I was very grateful for my older, wiser siblings. Although I knew better, it helped to have someone tell me that I needed to think more logically, because in this case I was lucky, very lucky, to have only a red neck and an aching head—which, by the way, they took pictures of at the station. I now know that if this incident were to happen again, I would be cooperative so I wouldn't get myself or others hurt.

Oh, and by the way, I found out that the tall man who hit me in the neck and head had already been convicted for rape, so the police and I felt pretty good that he was finally caught. Again, not enough to justify almost getting myself killed, but let me tell ya—my head and red neck felt a whole lot better after that.

* * *

We've all been asked, "Where were you on 9/11?" We've never really answered honestly, until now. The following five stories attempt to relate our interpretations of that day and our individual places in it.

9/11

BY DESIRAE BROWN

New York City
2001

Most New Yorkers tune into the radio station 1010 WINS for their news. I know this because I would most often hear 1010 WINS in a taxicab, at the deli, or in a convenience store. It had a very distinctive sound—at the start of every ten-minute show, instead of the usual intense-but-upbeat news-music that usually alerts one to the delivery of the news, the clacking of typewriter keys would snap loudly, and then dim a bit into the background as the announcer started in to drown them out. That incessant ticking always accompanied the news on 1010 WINS. I suppose we were to believe that an army of journalists, stationed at formica desks, wearing wide-lapelled suits, were updating the news at such a pace over there at 1010 WINS that the typewriters could not be stopped. I liked 1010 WINS. I got my news quickly and accurately when my radio alarm clock went off every morning in the dorms at Juilliard. Every morning, that is, until the day I stopped listening to 1010 WINS.

The last morning I tuned into 1010 WINS seemed like a normal day. I woke up, heard the weather and news as I climbed down from my bunk, and then showered. When I came back to my room, it was a little after nine o'clock in the morning. As I went about my business, I heard the familiar voice over the radio. The announcer's voice, so familiar after five years of living in New York, was strained as he stopped mid-sentence. "And we have some breaking news. I can't even believe this as I'm reading it, but it appears an airplane has flown into one of the towers of the World Trade Center."

I stopped. What? My brain couldn't even process what he was saying. The World Trade Center? I had friends and acquaintances who worked there. I had been there myself. What did this mean? Maybe this was a joke, like Orson Welles's "War of the Worlds." Somehow I thought it must not be that bad…. My reasoning was rejecting this as reality.

I continued dressing like it was a normal day. Then there was some banging on my door. Greg, my brother, was there.

"Did you hear about the World Trade Center?!" he asked, a little out of breath. "They're evacuating everybody in the dorm building. I hear we have like ten-fifteen minutes at the most to get out of here."

Again my mind wasn't accepting what I was hearing. "What do you mean?! Where are we supposed to go?" I asked in a panic.

"I don't know. They said everybody's supposed to meet in the Juilliard Theater because it's mostly underground. The R.A.s said the city is evacuating most of the tall buildings because they don't know if there's another target. Oh, and we're supposed to bring our pillows with us." *Target*?

"What do we need our pillows for?" I asked, totally confused.

Gregory paused a little at my question. "Well, in case we have to sleep there."

"Sleep there?! How long are we going to be evacuated? Should I pack up some stuff?" I knew I was being panicky, but I just needed some answers, and Greg seemed like the only one who had any at the moment.

"You don't have *time* to pack anything. I think we just have to go." He stopped. "I've got some binoculars in my room, and I saw the towers from my window. You can see the flames and everything, and there's junk flying everywhere in the air and…," he spoke haltingly, "and I think there might be people jumping out of the windows. I'm not sure." He added quietly, "It just looked like…people."

We stood silent for a moment. Things became clear then. I told Gregory I'd meet Melody and Deondra and him in the dorm lobby in a few minutes. Then I grabbed my pillow and a backpack. I looked around my room before I left and realized how quickly my reality could change. How quickly the things I was looking at could become meaningless.

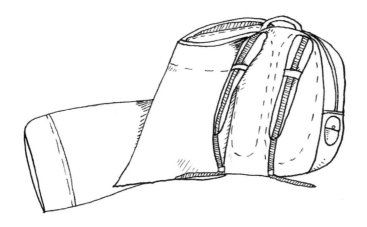

The four of us met in the lobby and made our way to the Juilliard Theater, along with a crush of other students. The seriousness of the situation hung heavily in the air and contrasted with the ridiculousness of the pillows in the students' arms.

"One of the towers fell while I was watching it out the window," Gregory said bluntly. I guess there was no other way to say it.

"It just fell?" I asked.

"It just fell, like with a bunch of smoke. It just fell straight down." There was nothing else to be said. We knew what it meant. People were dying. Maybe people we knew.

Once everyone was seated in the theater, I looked around. Everything had a different meaning now. All the past performances, all the legendary artists who got their start in this theater, now seemed like ghosts gracing the stage. Someone from the administration got up and stood near the first row of theater seats, in front of the famous stage. He announced, "We don't have very much information for you. We do know that both of the World Trade Center towers have been hit. The city has ordered us to evacuate any tall buildings or sites that can easily be targets from the sky. This includes the Lincoln Center. The Juilliard Theater is underground and will be a safe place for any who would choose to stay here until we hear that the dorm is safe for re-habitation. The city has also closed off all access in or out of the city, aside from emergency vehicles. This is all the information we have at this time." He paused. "The cafeteria staff will be arranging lunch in the theater lobby. We suggest that you stay here, though those who choose to may stay with friends that live uptown."

Everyone started murmuring. We were just supposed to stay there? Greg, Melody, and Deondra and I started talking amongst ourselves.

"I don't know if I want to stay here, guys. What if this lasts for days?" Greg started.

"Yeah," I agreed, "I don't want to wait around here. But where would we go?"

"Well, Dan and Katherine have a place uptown," said Melody. "Maybe we could call and see if they would let us stay with them."

Greg reached for his cell phone to dial their number. He put his phone to his ear and then dropped it back into his lap. "No cell phone service. I guess the cell phone towers were on top of the Trade Center. I called Mom and Dad right after the first one was hit. At least they know we're okay."

"Well, what are we going to do, just go uptown and show up on Dan and Katherine's doorstep?" Deondra asked."I guess so. What do you guys say?" I asked.

"I say let's go. It's probably going to take forever as it is to get a cab," Greg answered. Deondra and Melody agreed.

We gathered our bags and pillows and worked our way out of the theater. As we were passing through the lobby, I saw the cafeteria staff laying out an elaborate spread for lunch. Some students were hanging around waiting to serve themselves. I wondered if they should be laying out so much food; it seemed so much more than enough. New York City depends on numerous truckloads of food each day to keep the city fed. Because it is an island, and because it is built up so much, there isn't room to store a lot of food. Whatever is in a grocery store, or in a person's small storage space or refrigerator, is what is available. I remember wondering what the next few days would bring. My mind kept repeating the words, "There will be no access in or out of the city...." I wondered if I was being an alarmist, or if things were going to continue getting worse.

We walked out of the lobby doors and into the glaring sun on Broadway. There I saw the streets full of people, but no cars. There was no honking, no engines, no taxicab drivers yelling, or just saying hello to each other. Nobody was hailing a cab or chatting on the street corner. In fact, nobody was talking, yet thousands of people filled the void the cars had left. They were all walking, silently, covered in white powder, in the same direction. They were all walking the same direction we wanted to go. Uptown. We were millions of people trapped on a twenty-one-square-mile island, all trying to find "higher ground," all trying to escape the disaster wreaked on the streets of Lower Manhattan.

The five of us stood on the curb watching the unreal spectacle unfold before us. As I studied the people covered in powder, the reality of what was going on a few miles away from me began to take shape. What had these people seen, to be so covered in ash? Their faces were drawn, yet nearly expressionless. Shock and fatigue covered their countenances just as the powder and ash covered their bodies.

My mind reeled trying to reconcile what had happened, what was happening still as we stood frozen on the corner of 65th and Broadway. Later, I would see news broadcasts of what was happening at that moment, what these people had actually seen. Later, I would find out that the horrors I was imagining that moment were worse than I knew. Later, friends, nurses, and regular people alike would recount the blood and chaos they experienced. Yet part of me already knew what had happened by looking into the vacant faces of the silent pilgrimage before me.

Finally I broke the silence between the five of us. "Should we just start walking?" More silence.

"Look at the bus stop," somebody finally said. We all turned our gaze to the next corner on the left. There were hundreds of people forming a thick line leading down the block from the bus stop. Considering that maybe fifty people could squeeze onto a bus, and obviously a bus hadn't arrived in some time, it seemed that taking the bus uptown was out of the question. I couldn't see any buses anywhere up or down the street, so what were these people waiting for?

"I guess we're just going to have to start walking," Greg said.

"It's going to be a long walk all the way uptown," I added.

"Yeah, I don't know guys," Melody joined in. "With these crowds it could take hours."

Then we noticed our church, the Church of Jesus Christ of Latter-day Saints, across the street from us. We saw that their doors were open. Actually, I think Deondra saw it first.

"Hey, guys, I think the church is open."

"You sure?" I asked. "Looks like everything is shut down. I don't think anyone's sticking around."

"No, really. I think the door is open," she insisted. Broadway widens quite a bit at 65th, so the front of the church was still off in the distance.

"Hey, I think you're right," Greg added. We all agreed we should go check it out.

So with pillows in hand, we crossed the street and entered the open doorway of the church. I vaguely remember someone being there to greet us.

But then my memory gives out. Like a blackout, my subconscious snatched the next hours from my life.

As I'm writing this, I realize I really don't know what happened after we walked into the church. I am tempted to call my sister and ask her what we ended up doing, where we waited out the day until we were able to return to the dorms. But I stop myself. I know that I must have felt safe after I realized someone was there to take care of me. As strange as it sounds, I guess that was part of my experience. Somewhere the missing hours are floating, but I can't find them.

The next thing I remember was being back in my dorm room at night. I was sitting on the window ledge, looking out at the city. I sat there for a long time and listened to the unfamiliar silence. I had grown so accustomed to hearing commercial airplanes constantly flying over the city that it was a bit disorienting to hear nothing. Every fifteen minutes or so, an F-16 would rumble overhead and break the quiet. The first time I heard one fly over, it frightened me; it seemed to be flying so low. I soon realized that the growling fighter planes had people in them who were protecting us, and I felt relief. As I looked out over that vast tangle of city, I wondered that I would feel so claustrophobic. Nobody was getting in or out of that city, and I couldn't get any calls in or out either. That understanding kept spinning through my mind. Though I wasn't going to try to go anywhere, I knew I was trapped. My parents and Ryan were far away in Utah, and I was bothered by the thought that I couldn't communicate with them—let alone go see them.

Life was strange over the next few days. The fighter planes were the only things flying overhead, and the wind shifted the next day, blowing smoke and a strange smell over the city. We commented on the smell and felt like we were walking around in a fog. Every lamppost and city corner had missing-persons flyers tacked up by the hundreds. There was a fire station directly behind Juilliard, and I remember stopping by the shrines of pictures, candles, and flowers. I looked at the faces of those lost, and cried for their families. As I walked the streets, I would see other New Yorkers doing the same. The strangest thing in those days following 9/11 was the way that New Yorkers interacted with each other. I had never previously, in my New York years, had a stranger just start talking to me as though I were a friend. New Yorkers don't usually trust so easily. Strangers were talking to strangers. It was like the city was transformed. This lasted for a few days, maybe a week, and then life slid back to normal.

Regrettably, soon everyone was again moving through the city as though in an invisible cocoon, as usual. And again, people resumed pretending not to see one another.

Everyone who knows I lived in New York City asks where I was on 9/11. I wasn't down at Ground Zero, and I don't feel like I helped anyone. I was just one of the millions of New Yorkers who happened to live in the city that day. I am one of the millions who know what existence is like when reality is stripped from you, and the bare bones of your life are exposed. And I am one of the millions who probably try not to relive those moments. Once you relive them, as I am doing now, the protected life we live feels fragile and fleeting.

Strangely, even now, if I run out the door without hearing the news, I panic just a little that maybe a disaster may have occurred, and I just don't know about it. All these years later, I still listen for commercial airplanes because if they are flying, I know everything must be okay. Even still, there is a place in the very back of my mind that is frightened that life, and security, will be stripped from me again, and I may never be able to find it.

* * *

THROUGH THE LOOKING GLASS

BY GREGORY BROWN

**The Juilliard Dorms
New York City
September 11, 2001**

I couldn't believe what I had just seen. Turning to the elevator behind me, I impatiently pushed the "up" button over and over again. It's a total pet peeve of mine when people do that, thinking it's gonna make the dang thing come faster, but at this moment, I didn't realize what I was doing. After waiting in the dorm lobby for what seemed like ages, the little white light finally flashed on the elevator nearest me, and the doors opened. I hurried in while the current passengers were still getting off—another huge New York no-no—and started mashing on "19" just as I had the previous button.

"In a rush?" jeered a fellow pianist, who had evidently noticed my eccentric behavior.

"Just look out the window toward downtown; you'll see," I yelled back through the closing doors.

Upon reaching the nineteenth floor, I squeezed through the half-open elevator doors and started toward my dorm-room suite. Before turning the final corner, I saw a crowd of people packed into the small R.A. lounge across the hall from my suite. Distracted by this unusual gathering, I turned into the lounge instead. Through the door, I nudged my way a little further into the room, trying to get a better look at the center of the crowd's attention, only to have my heart jump into my throat. Screams of very real terror rang through the air as everyone stared in disbelief at the TV in front of them. There were so many people in there that I couldn't maneuver around and get a good look at the screen, but the cries of astonishment finally let up enough to where I could pick out a few words from the news broadcaster.

At first I thought I must have heard wrong. There's no way those words could possibly have been the truth! After a moment vacant of thought, I regained my senses and remembered my purpose for coming back up to the nineteenth floor. I squished my way out of the crowd and ran across the hall to my dorm room. Once I got control of the keys in my hand, I shut the door behind me and took a deep breath.

I knew what I had come up here to get, but now I wasn't so sure I wanted to. Waffling, I walked over to my bed, under which a small white cardboard box lay, and I stood there debating whether I really wanted to see more. Gaining a little nerve, I reached my hand underneath the bunk-board and felt the box against my fingers. As I began pulling it out, the immense reality of what was happening outside flooded my heart, and emotion got the better of me. My hand dropped to the carpet below, my knees quickly followed suit, and before I knew it I was overcome by tearful prayer.

"God, be with them—be with their families."

What more can you really pray for in such a moment? I wiped my eyes, partially regained my composure, and slowly pulled out the box. There they were, right where I knew they'd be, sitting atop a bunch of junk that had accumulated over a little more than a year of classes and homework. I don't know why I chose to bring them from home the previous year, because they didn't serve much of a purpose in such a cramped city. After blowing off a thin layer of dust, I unzipped the case and took them out. They were already adjusted for my eyes, so the focus of the lenses didn't need much tweaking. I got to my feet, took a few steps over to the window, and lifted them to my eyes.

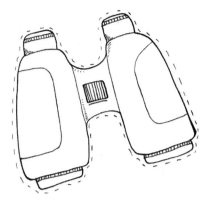

Sure enough, where only hours before two bright pillars reached over the morning horizon, there now stood only one—one lonely mast floating on a cloud of dark gray. I stood there in silence, watching this solitary sentinel as violent flames consumed his belly and his most precious living tears dropped to the ground below. I could feel his sadness, I could see his pain, and as he wept, far less priceless treasures fell from my own eyes. I can't say how many minutes the two of us had together that morning—sharing in each other's grief, trying to comprehend the magnitude of each other's sorrow, connected by a mere dusty, old looking glass—but as he too sank deep into the growing sea of gray, joining his already conquered companion, a little piece of my soul, of my innocence, of my carefree youth was lost along with him.

The gray waves more and more greedily consumed the bright sky above, as even the sun was forced to veil its face in mourning. I lowered the lenses from my dampened eyes, re-zipped them into their case, and slid the box back under my bed. There were no more thoughts to be had, there were no more tears to be shed; there was nothing left but the beating of my own heart and the sound of life in my shallow breath. I glanced back over to the window reluctantly, and there amidst the thick gloom was a faint circle of light breaking through the deep gray. The sun always seems to shine a little brighter on the darkest of days.

A faint hum from my pocket gently broke the spell.

"Hello?"

"Yeah, Dad, I'm all right. The girls and I didn't go downtown this morning."

* * *

INNOCENTS

BY DEONDRA BROWN

New York City
September 11, 2001

"This is not a joke," quipped my favorite morning radio station DJ. "An airplane has just crashed into the side of one of the World Trade Center towers." Playing practical jokes and making gullible people believe crazy things is just part of the life of a radio host, but today was different. Today there wasn't even a tinge of sarcasm. My mind raced as I immediately flipped the station to 1010 WINS, New York's most respected FM news authority.

I heard a confirmation of the most disturbing and shocking news of my life. Somehow it was true, even though it seemed impossible. I immediately grabbed my cell phone and dialed my parents back home in Utah. It couldn't have been much later than 6 a.m. there, but I didn't care. My dad answered after a couple of rings, and it was apparent that I had awakened them. In a few brief words I explained volumes, and he ran to flip on the television. Just then the other tower was hit.

My parents knew that being five miles away from the Twin Towers was pretty far in New York City blocks, and so told the four of us in the city—Ryan was home in Utah—to stick together and that we'd talk again later. There was no immediate threat to our safety, and so we agreed to keep them informed. I threw something on other than pajamas and ran downstairs to the dorm's common room, where the big television was already on. I joined dozens of others crowded around the screen who had tuned in only a few moments before. Then it happened—the first tower began to crumble, and just as quickly, it was gone. Shrieks and gasps filled the air as we all realized the magnitude of what was happening. Our little bubble of security had been burst, and I was certain our lives would never be the same again.

Students who had gone years as strangers without uttering a word to one another were now crying together and hugging, as we all sought for some sort of comfort amidst so much pain and sorrow. Others just sat there, frozen in time from fear and disbelief. There was the most disturbing silence I had ever heard. Even the television, though still broadcasting, seemed to go silent. No one knew what to do. There were no words to describe what was happening.

The time that passed seemed only an instant. We were all still somehow glued to the television, struggling to see through tear-clouded eyes, all wondering the same thing and hoping and praying it could be true: that all those people on a busy weekday morning had somehow gotten out. It had to be true. It just had to.

Gregory said he could see the second tower burning from his window using his binoculars. I ran to see, needing a much-needed escape from the reality of the news with the vision of the falling tower forever implanted in my mind. It was true. The flames were as visible as if watching them on TV, except that this was even more eerie. This was reality.

No one had moved, or I suspect even spoken, while I had left the common room to view the flames. Upon returning, I looked aside for a brief second before hearing the all-too-familiar shrieks. And before I knew it, the second tower was gone too, just like the first, crumbling floor-upon-floor as it raced to the ground. The fear was overwhelming and crippling now. Although I was miles away, I was afraid for our well-being. All were afraid of what was going to be the next target.

Cell phone service was down. The antennas had been atop the now deceased towers. Pay phones were jammed and thus unreliable because of the excess of callers. Everyone was

LIFE BETWEEN THE KEYS

left on his or her own to wonder the fate of their loved ones. We felt blessed that we had spoken to my parents so early that morning. Many families were left panic-stricken.

With Juilliard being a part of the Lincoln Center complex, we were ordered by the mayor to evacuate within thirty minutes. Mayor Giuliani was rightfully nervous of more attacks and asked for well-known city locations and tall buildings to be vacated. We were told by our advisors to grab a pillow and some blankets and immediately report to the basement of our school for further directions. We might not be allowed back in our rooms for some time. No one knew for sure.

We did precisely as we were told, but there were no concrete "further directions" anyone could offer us. No one knew what the mayor's next move would be. I wonder if he even knew. Pillows and blankets in hand, we left our shelter and ventured outside. We contemplated our options for a few moments before deciding to walk across the street to our Mormon church. Maybe they would be opening their doors for refuge.

The scene was nothing short of amazing: masses of people covered from head to toe in ashes and dust, solemnly and quietly walking uptown. No cars on the road, just people covering the streets; no one speaking. Dozens upon dozens of grief-stricken people working their way uptown to get away from it all, as far away as possible. But their clothes and the looks on their faces said it all. There was no escaping. Their eyes had been opened in such a way that life for them would forever be changed: tainted and scarred.

We were told at the Mormon church that nothing was set up quite yet, but that before night there would be accommodations made for anyone who needed sanctuary. We felt safer with the thought of staying the night in a church instead of the basement of our school. We knew we would be safe there if we weren't allowed back to our rooms.

With nowhere else to turn at the moment and our blankets getting heavy, we decided to head back to Juilliard. We were told upon returning to our school basement that the mayor had removed the evacuation order, and that we were free to return to our rooms. We dropped off our bedding and decided it was time to get something to eat. No one had even thought much about the fact that we'd gone all day without food. There were much more pressing things on our minds, and I think the images ingrained in our heads from the day had taken any urge to eat away completely.

Our favorite diner was somehow open, with the familiar waitress much more friendly and courteous than usual. We were all in this together, no matter how we got here. She must have felt the same. Upon ordering, I spotted an available pay phone just outside the restaurant. It was worth a shot. I tried over and over again. All circuits would forever be busy, it seemed. I decided to try one more time, noticing a beckoning from inside the restaurant that my food had arrived. Before I was aware, the phone was ringing on the other end.

Dad knew it was us. His caller ID had spotted the 212 area code. He was glad to hear my voice, as I was to hear his. I quickly recounted the events of the day, not sure how many minutes our scrounged-up change would get me. He and Mom were glad to have spoken with us before we were unreachable. Their phone had been ringing off the hook all day long from friends, neighbors, distant friends, and associates—anyone and everyone, it seemed—all knowing they had four children in New York and wondering if we were okay. We'd never realized so many people cared.

I don't know a person anywhere who can't remember exactly where they were when they first heard about the towers that day. And most importantly, how they felt. We were blessed to have one another. We knew that amidst such inconceivable events, we had built-in support and several shoulders to cry on. I will forever remember the innocents who lost their lives, the families who are left to pick up the pieces, and the unexpected heroes along the way. Those of us left behind physically survived, but we will *never* forget how it felt to be there, and who we are now because of it. A deep and permanent scar will forever linger as a reminder.

✳   ✳   ✳

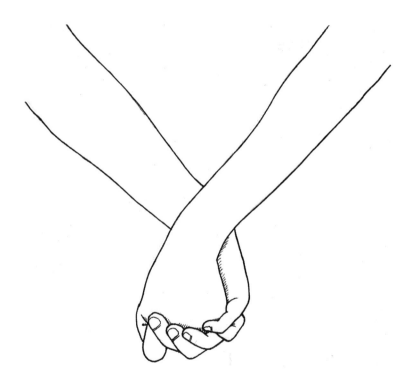

GROUND ZERO: A MEMORY FROM THE SKY

BY RYAN BROWN

New York City
September 11, 2001

When I was sixteen, I was the only one out of the five of us who moved back to Utah from New York with my parents. My other four siblings stayed in New York to attend college at Juilliard. By this time, I was in my fourth year at the Juilliard Pre-College, having no choice but to fly back and forth from Utah to New York. Pre-College is a division of the school that's held once a week for junior high and high school students who want to receive some of the best training in music. My life revolved around Pre-College. It all seemed so routine, until one day...

Crack! The sound of my door jolted me out of my dreams.

"Ryan, the Twin Towers are on fire!" Dad yelled and ran back to the TV in the living room. I sprinted from bed, almost falling over in the process because my eyes were still blurry from sleeping. Looking at the TV, I saw the two familiar towers in New York on fire. Questions of disbelief popped into my head. I ended up asking my dad 500 questions about how this had happened.

"I don't know, I just turned on the TV, but I think I heard that it was a terrorist attack," he told me.

My jaw dropped. I couldn't believe what I was seeing and hearing. As my dad and I stared for hours at the news, we remembered that I had a flight scheduled for

September 12. My stomach fell at the thought of being included in the disaster of September 11. It was scary to think how close I was to flying on that day.

Twenty-four hours had passed and everything seemed so different. It was as if people were lost in trying to find reality. Things were quiet; people were reserved and glued to their televisions, wishing that the events of September 11 had never taken place. I just couldn't watch it anymore! There was just too much sadness. All I could do was practice and get ready to fly to New York for school. The airports had been closed two days, with no sign of reopening soon. People were stranded there with no end in sight.

I was anxious to get to New York and make sure my siblings and friends were okay. I was waiting for word of airports reopening, which finally came on September 14. The airports were up and running, but no flights were going out! I couldn't figure out why. Later I found out that airlines were still too scared to let any planes fly. It wasn't until nighttime that I got a call from my airline telling me that they finally rescheduled my flight to New York. The airline I used was only about a year old, but I heard they were the first to put armored-cockpit doors in their planes.

The airport felt like a ghost town. The only people around were janitors mopping the floors and picking up trash.

"Oh, hi, Ryan. Good to see you again. Out for classes?" the lady at the ticket counter said.

"Good to see you too, Jen. Yeah, I'm heading back to New York for classes. I can't believe this airline is the first to have planes fly out."

"I know, the flight you're on tonight is one of the first three since it happened," she responded.

"Wow, I just can't believe that." I paused, and then my reservation about flying came out. "You think the flight's going to be safe?"

"Yes," she said, "it should be. Security has been heightened, and they're checking people extremely well."

Relieved, I said, "Awesome."

The security checkpoint was a bit nerve-racking because I knew they would check everything. I hoped I didn't have anything suspicious that would jeopardize my flight to New York. I didn't worry too much because I knew many of the security guards, due to my frequent flights.

When I passed through security, the airport remained barren. All of the airport stores were closed, and there was only one other person walking toward the gate. As I boarded, I was stunned to see only twenty or so passengers.

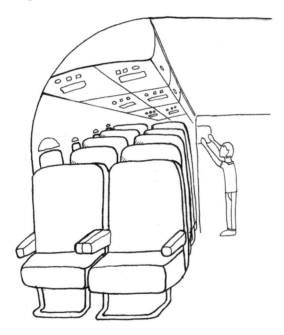

This freaked me out because I had never seen a plane so empty. I walked past a few rows until I found one entirely empty so I could lie down for a good night's sleep. What seemed like five minutes later, I heard the captain's voice over the intercom saying that we were landing soon, and also that he had been granted permission to fly over Ground Zero. I immediately sat up to look out the window and saw that we were insanely close to the buildings around us. Smoke surrounded us, clouding our vision. Circling the site, I could see the wreckage still smoldering and the crews and vehicles working at finding survivors. I don't consider myself a particularly emotional person, but I found myself getting teary-eyed. I looked around the cabin and saw the same emotion on the rest of passengers.

Walking around New York seemed so foreign to me that week. It was strange to see police, army men, and army vehicles patrolling the streets, but one of the biggest changes I remember is how different people seemed. People were no longer caught up in their own worlds of business or school. There was more love and compassion for one another. Getting in a cab or being on the subway, I noticed people were much more friendly, more connected. They just wanted to help one another in any way they could. Even though this was a hard time for Americans, it was good to know that people could come together as one.

✳   ✳   ✳

MAN-MADE BEAUTY

BY MELODY BROWN

New York City
September 2001

With the loud music and distraction of hot new freshmen, it was hard to see even beyond the rusted metal of the boat. And the whole point of the Hudson River cruise was to enable us to get past the metal and concrete walls of our city dorm. Rarely did we get to see New York City from the outside, since 65th Street was our sole attraction.

Every year as part of the Juilliard School's orientation, a big dance party is held on a harbor cruise before school starts. This year I was a sophomore in college, feeling a bit older and more confident at seventeen. The bulk of my scenic trip was spent sending flirtatious glances to guys I didn't know. My sight was wrapped up in "good-looking guy near the pole" when in the middle of a strategic bypass the boat pushed me into the railing instead of my prospect. The breath was knocked out of my vanity, but for the first time I saw what I'll forever remember: man-made beauty.

These were the only words that came to mind. Somehow the beautiful setting sun and clear blue sky only sufficed as a backdrop. In front of me were two of the most magnificent buildings I had ever seen. Stealing the orange glow of the sun, they turned into golden pillars of light. I was in awe; I had seen them so many times before, but never like this. The idea that men made those towers was inspiring. Even from the distance of the river, they dwarfed all that was around them. I was suddenly proud of the flesh and bones that housed an intellect inside me. I felt indestructible being part of a great civilization in such an opportune time.

Although the moment was fleeting, the pride in humankind made my heart swell. It was the first time I had such profound respect for man, and the only time when I felt praising God would be unjust. This was what *we* could do; this is what *I* can do. Not even a week later, everything would change.

Awakened by the blare of my roommate's scrambled Spanish station, I started the day yelling. Of course, I was only drowned out by radio static. Within half an hour, another commotion—sirens were going crazy outside. I didn't think much about it until I started putting on my makeup. Facing the window for the best source of light, I wondered why there were people on the roof across from me. It started with two who were animatedly talking and pointing. Gradually came five, then ten, then twenty, all pointing the same way. The sirens broke out of my subconscious, and right then I knew something was wrong.

I turned on the radio, but the Top 40 station was for once playing music. I started trying to find the news channels when there was a knock at the door. The R.A. said one thing: "You HAVE to come see this." She led me to a suite I'd never seen before. Here a huge window framed what people all over the city were pointing at. One of the towers was on fire, the black smoke already billowing over Lower Manhattan. I froze. Those were flames coming out of a building that housed thousands of workers. I *had* to go upstairs and find my siblings. This was not good.

I went first to Gregory's room, finding Deondra there as well. He had been putting my dad's binoculars to use, sickened by what he was seeing. Frantically he told me, "There are people jumping out of the building!" At this point we knew we needed more information. How was this happening?

Gregory lived on the floor with the R.A. lounge, which had a television. The door to the lounge was open, and we heard as we walked in:

"An airplane seems to have hit the first tower. We were filming the aftermath when a second plane, here you can see it, comes around and crashes into the other tower. The footage you're seeing now shows our reporter in front of the burning tower when suddenly, without any warning, this tower falls. It's hard to see through the huge amounts of dust, but it has fallen. Firefighters are trying to save the second tower. We have reports that the Pentagon has been hit as well."

I looked at Deondra; she had tears in her eyes as she took in the immensity of the news. In the split second I looked away came "OH, MY GOODNESS!" and my eyes snapped back to the television, "WE THINK THE SECOND TOWER HAS JUST FALLEN!" There was so much dust and smoke that again no one could understand what had just happened. At this point the R.A.s received a phone call.

One said, "They're evacuating all of the high rises and landmarks." We were both; the dorm was part of Lincoln Center and a high rise. "We've got to move fast. Take blankets and pillows, nothing else," the R.A. continued.

I ran down to my room and grabbed the only blanket I had, my huge feather-filled comforter. The elevators were out of service so I had to run down the stairs blinded, my gigantic comforter blocking everything in front of me. Adrenaline moved me extremely fast. Before I'd realized, I had run down twenty flights of stairs carrying massive amounts of feathers.

Being shuffled out of the dorm building and into the school meant I was now in the lobby of Juilliard barely dressed, holding the makings of my bed. This truly was a nightmare. Nothing felt real. We found our main piano teacher in the lobby, who was just as stunned as we were. Most everyone in the school building didn't have access to a television, so she had only heard rumors of what happened. We were in the middle of informing her when she turned to me with a confused look. "Why are you holding such a big comforter?"

"I don't know. They told us to bring pillows and blankets. This was all I had."

She quietly said, "Oh, okay," and walked off in a daze.

The loud, monotone school officials then had our attention: "Please make your way down to the Juilliard Theater. Being below ground with no windows is the safest place right now. We will have the cafeteria bring in lunch for everyone."

It's as though someone knocked me out at this second. My memory starts again at the meridian walkway between Broadway and Columbus Avenue. It was so hot; I couldn't carry my enormous comforter anymore. Gregory had it and looked extremely irritated. We were all so confused. The subway was down, the bus system was down, and cabs were trying to get out of the city. We were attempting to get to our friends' apartment uptown, but we soon found it was impossible. If people were walking miles from the horrific scene in business suits and heels, there was no way we were going anywhere. Droves were making their way from downtown, each telling his or her own story through tears, dust-covered faces, and bloodstained clothes.

Seeing the streets filled with thousands of aimless people left me speechless. We didn't belong there; we felt it. This was a hallowed place for those suffering. Intruding on moments of raw personal vulnerability made me realize that I wasn't a fellow victim, just an onlooker witnessing severe pain.

Suddenly nothing was important anymore. The city tried to move on, but it had been brutally crippled. My own little Juilliard community was taking it incredibly hard. The drama students in particular couldn't function anymore. We later attributed the breakdown to artists' emotions being constantly on the surface.

I would walk the halls in awe of such students collapsing in tears. I thought, "Why don't I feel like that? Do I even care?" It all just seemed unreal, as if I were in the latest apocalyptic movie.

Months went by and eventually the non-victims began to forget. Grades, relationships, practicing, and mundane life took over again. I was impressed and almost disturbed that nothing affected me. That is, until the first dream woke me up in a panic.

From the view of an airplane, I could see the city. I was in the copilot's chair, looking out the large windows, when almost directly below I beheld an enormous stadium. The lights were on, a game taking place, filling the stadium to capacity. Suddenly the plane banked steeply, and I was lying on top of the window to my side. I felt us dropping, the roar stifling my screams. We were crashing into the stadium below, my hands and body propped up against the window. "No!" I could see thecrowd of thousands coming so clearly into sight; we were about to crash!

I woke up. Right then I knew it had only been a matter of time before the numbness subsided. Waking up crying became normal. Night after night I would have dreams of my city being destroyed. There would be fire and nuclear weapons; dreams where I couldn't find my family before the destruction.

I felt so weak and powerless. Every night I would have no control over my collapsing surroundings. Nothing was permanent or enduring, for it was all man-made.

One of the last dreams I would have came almost two years later. My world again was burning around me. I had a couple of minutes to take my last things. What I found most important, I placed in a little red wagon. I stacked my journals, my scriptures, and my beloved childhood stuffed companion, "Eddie." My siblings were at my side while we ran out of the city. I awoke.

Instead of waking up in tears, I was surprisingly peaceful. The things I had subconsciously chosen to bring with me *were* the most important things in my life. For in my journals were the invaluable personal truths I had found in life, religion, and philosophy. In my scriptures were the most profound, holy, and inspiring words that gave life purpose.

With my most beloved stuffed animal, "Guardian Angel Bear" (which was inscribed on her belly), I had found a childhood companion of safety, peace, and happiness. And lastly, at my side were my siblings.

These were the things that mattered. Despite whatever man-made buildings fell around me, I knew deep down that no one could take away my eternity. For after things have rusted and crumbled, what is left? I know within me is a soul where the truths I've learned, the memories I've lived, and the God I've found are eternal. And I hope, like in the dream, my family will be right by my side. Eternity would be nothing without them.

✳   ✳   ✳

The moments in between our practice sessions growing up were maybe more important to the creation of our family group than the actual practicing. The relationships we formed and fostered over the years have enabled us to work and play together as adults. Many people ask, "How can the five of you spend so much time together and not get sick of each other?" This story attempts to answer that question.

MARCUS

BY DESIRAE BROWN

Houston, Texas
Christmas, 1989

Some possessions are really precious to us. I think most people have mementos or heirlooms that hold memories and feelings far more significant than the objects themselves. Those emotions become real and vivid again every time we turn the thing over in our hands. As children we haven't had enough life experience, usually, to connect memories with objects. Even so, I remember creating strong attachments to certain things. I knew kids who had blankies or dolls they wouldn't leave home without. I had stuffed animals I loved and depended on for friendship and to fall asleep with at night in the dark.

In fact, most of my brothers and sisters adored stuffed animals. They were such real people to us. We knew, without a doubt, that they jumped to life the minute we shut the door on them, or let our eyes droop to sleep. There were times when we were supposed to be practicing the piano but wouldn't. Instead, one or more of us would sneak into the others' practice rooms to play. On these occasions we would make our stuffed animals come alive. Our "stufft-ies," as we called them, lived in a vibrant and exciting world. Their personalities were dramatic and oversized versions of us. We were sure that if we spent any time away from them while practicing that we would miss some new event in their ongoing saga. And a saga it was. There were stuffed animal wrestling matches, birthday parties, feuds, and weddings. For special occasions we would pull out every stuffed animal in the house and set them on every piece of furniture we could find, including bookshelves, televisions, and the ping-pong table. We didn't want anyone to miss out on the fun. There was also a hierarchy, with leaders among the popular stuffed animals. And all of the stufft-ies had names.

The most fun and dramatic of the animal people were the hippopotamuses. Gregory, Melody, and Ryan all had hippopotamuses that were the favorites of the stufft-ie world. There was Tip, or Tippy, by all standards the most popular of the hippos. Tip had a high, funny voice and made everyone laugh all the time. There was also Baybay, who was smaller than Tip and therefore the "baby" hippo. She was Melody's favorite. Because Melody had a bit of a speech impediment when she was little, so did Baybay. Then there was Cleo, Ryan's hippo with a pink bowtie, whose unfortunate female name—for a boy hippo—was given him by Gregory. Ryan initially cried and whined at the name, but soon lost interest in the argument, and the name stuck. Because Ryan was the youngest, Cleo was always a little crazy. He said wild things and was always ready to pick a fight. I had a stuffed bunny, Mr. Bunny, whom I loved, but I always wished that I had a hippo like everyone else. Everyone else, that is, except Deondra. She never quite understood our fascination with the stufft-ies. She stuck to her Barbies and her practicing.

One day a brilliant bright-blue hippo, with a blue satin bow around his neck, joined the household. Our Grandmom had seen Tip come to her house on visits and thought he was getting a bit old and needed a new friend. She loved to give nice gifts and bought the new hippo as an early Christmas present for Gregory. This fancy hippo was bought at Neiman Marcus, so we all thought that Marcus was the perfect name for him. Marcus kind of intimidated the other hippos at first, being so plush and perfect, but soon everyone liked him. Especially me. I didn't have a hippo, and he was so pretty. I secretly wished he were mine. Mr. Bunny and Marcus became very good friends. Gregory must have noticed how much I liked him. Even though Marcus was Gregory's second-favorite after Tip, he let me borrow him quite a bit. Sometimes I even got to line up Marcus in my bed next to Mr. Bunny and keep him overnight. We always slept with all of our stuffed animals every night, so to lend out a favorite was a special kindness.

Christmas morning came, and as usual the five of us met very early in the morning before we woke our parents. Even as tiny kids we would exchange little presents. One of us would wake up first in the very dim early morning and quietly nudge the others awake one by one. We knew Mom and Dad wouldn't let us open Santa's presents until it was light out, so this was our way of playing together until we could be "legally" awake. We would whisper and try to muffle laughter while anticipating the happiest day of the year. Then we would gather around the little two-foot-tall Christmas tree that my parents let us keep in the room I shared with my two sisters. In the small glow from the colored Christmas lights we would give each other miniature presents of candy or yo-yos. We'd hidden these gifts from one another until Christmas Eve, when we would sneak them under our little tree during the night.

On this particular Christmas morning, there were the usual small, oddly wrapped presents, of course, but also an orange box next to the tree. It was the kind of box a person bought oranges in at Christmastime. We all sat Indian-style around the mini-tree and began one by one to share our gifts. It was so sweet to know that my brother or sister had thought about me and used their own money to get me a gift they thought I would like. We each felt such joy at seeing the others' reactions to the gifts and then expressing gratitude for them.

After all the smaller gifts had been opened, Gregory got a sneaky smile on his face. Then, while reaching around to pull the orange box forward, he said, "There's one more present, though. Hey, Fat, this is for you." Fat was my nickname because pictures showed that I had been a chubby baby.

As Gregory pushed the box toward me, I felt bad about getting the biggest present and flustered. "I don't need such a big present!" I said, though I was excited about it and reached for the gift. There was no wrapping paper because Gregory didn't know how to wrap presents. The sweetness of him trying to think of a way to package the gift touched me. I pulled the present toward me, then slowly slid the top off the box and set it aside. I looked inside and was motionless at what I saw. My heart felt like it was going to explode. There, smashed inside the box, was Marcus. Of the few possessions in Gregory's life, he was giving me one of his most prized. I sat staring at Marcus in disbelief. Then tears started to blur my vision as I looked up at Gregory and said, "Oh, Gregory, you don't have to give him to me! I could just borrow him for a while...." Not only was Gregory giving me Marcus, the stuffed hippo, but he was also giving me the privilege of being Marcus's voice and personality. He was giving away his friend.

"No, I want you to have him," he said with a sweet smile. He was happy to see me so moved by the gift, but, knowing him so well, I knew there was a part of him that was mourning the loss. This made the gift even more meaningful. I reached over to Gregory and hugged him. In our childhood language there was no way to really express what we were feeling, what had just been exchanged between us.

Looking back now as an adult, I wonder if I will ever give a gift of that magnitude, if I will ever be able to give the way that Gregory did. All I know is that it was one of the greatest gifts I will ever receive. I wish, strangely, that everyone could feel how I felt that Christmas morning, when my brother gave me nearly all he had.

* * *